Re-membering in the
Shadows

Re-membering in the Shadows

SANTOS BOOKS

First Printing, 2025
Published by Santos Books LLC, Elizabethtown, PA
ISBN: 979-8-9928907-9-2

To the Authors of these stories

CONTENTS

Editor's Introduction

Just over three years ago, I audaciously asked Walter Brueggemann if I could write his biography. And perhaps, with some naivete, he agreed. Of course, I had no idea what I was in for. I only knew that I needed his story, and later I would learn that perhaps he needed it written. "I see my life as a whole more than I've seen it before," Walter remarked, as we read the last draft together. "I understand now that each teacher I had was providentially appointed."

Following the biography, I was asked by Carey Newman of Fortress Press to serve as Walter's editor on six more projects. Three have been released and three are forthcoming.

In the winter of 2024-25, I underwent Deep Brain Stimulation surgery for Parkinson's Disease. I had been diagnosed at the age of 52, seven years prior. Whether it was the effects of pain medication or some unexpected result of the surgery, I sensed a call to begin allowing others to tell their stories.

So with my wife Heidi's blessing and encouragement, Santos Books LLC was born. In 2025, we anticipate publishing approximately two dozen books, with most being memoirs, although not all.

In addition to editing and publishing books, I also lead workshops on writing. The essays in this collection represent a new twist--publishing the stories of the "students" who registered for the seven-session course. As you will see from the biographies of the writers, many are also writing for Santos Books.

The course had twenty students. While eleven students ultimately submitted essays, everyone in the class made a significant contribution. For if we learn to become human by being among others, we also learn to write by being with others.

As was true for the course, these essays will cause you to reflect, cry, laugh, and more! Most have to do with childhood memories, now filtered through many decades that have passed. And with such filtering, the truth is even more stark and real than we so often understood at the moment when we experienced the events of the story.

If you have an interest in writing for Santos Books or taking one of our writing courses, contact Conrad Kanagy at kanagy.conrad@gmail.com.

One

Childhood

By Lee Lever

As a young boy, I could only reach so far into the spring opening, fearful of what might be lurking there. The cold water bubbling up through the rocks numbed my hand and flowed into the creek, littered with stones to impede erosion. For hours, I played at the spring, stacking and rearranging the stones, reinforcing them with mud, watching the water rise and spill over, strangely satisfied by my efforts. Eventually, I walked the field road a quarter mile back home to the white farmyard buildings refreshed and at peace.

Corn grew tall in the rich black soil of Northern Illinois. Spring and summer rains were right on time, and the winters were cold. The spacious dairy barn, built with massive beams, was home to large black and white cows, suckling calves, mows of hay bales, and overflowing bins of corn and oats. A clutter of farm cats stalked mice and drank foamy milk poured into a milk can lid at milking time. The territorial farm dogs barked at and chased every vehicle down the lane to the gravel road where dust plumes marked the comings and goings of rural travelers.

The graveled center of the farmyard diverged in three directions; two dirt roads led out to the fields, and the graveled main driveway curved up the hill to the two-story house with a fork opposite to the second floor of the main barn. The farmyard hub was surrounded by dairy barn, milkhouse, silo, equipment sheds, shop, corn granaries, small barn, feed lots, cattle sheds, and another small pasture where sheep grazed. At the center, my father worked, taking care of farm business, talking with neighbors and visitors, and overseeing my work.

At age fourteen, my father broke his right arm when he fell from a loaded hayrack pulled by a team of horses. The doctors wanted to amputate his broken arm, but my grandfather would not allow it. After surgery, the arm healed, but Dad had limited bending range and bore a large scar on the inside bend of his elbow. Because of that limitation, he learned to eat left-handed and played the accordion upside down. The arm kept him out of the military and World War 2.

We were a musical family. My oldest sister played the accordion, and my next-oldest sister played marimba. I took lessons on the marimba for a while, but I did not become as proficient as my disciplined sibling. She still plays her marimba, providing the prelude and accompanying hymns at her church. My younger sister played the trumpet, and my mother played the violin. I would sing when our family gave programs in church and mission settings.

Our family traveled to the Pacific Garden Mission in Chicago to give musical programs. The marimba and accordion were always an attraction. My father was a lay preacher on those occasions.

Men came to the mission for a meal and a place to sleep. The rules were no drinking and a requirement to attend a worship service where the revivalist style prevailed. The mission walls displayed well-known Bible verses. Mission superintendent Harry Saulnier (Hallelujah Harry) walked up and down the aisles of the seated group, pleading and exhorting the men to turn to Jesus. His appeal was emotional. The responses were equally emotional as men wept and prayed for forgiveness. Harry probably saved my soul, but more importantly, modeled a man who cared deeply for the well-being of others.

My first memory of church was a Bible church with a woman preacher who played the trumpet. Pastor Helen was an oddity in my childhood's conservative, evangelical culture. My father often fell asleep during the service. It was strange to see him dressed up, sitting with the family in a pew. I was used to him being in bib overalls, working on the farm.

My second memory of church was the Meadowdale Gospel Chapel, a Plymouth Brethren congregation located in one of the first far-west suburbs of Chicago. Our family's musical skills were often on display there. I was six years old when I sang "Everybody Ought To Know" in front of the congregation. I almost fainted. Afterward, someone told me, "You sure sing loud." My sister and I also played a marimba duet.

My third memory of church was another Bible Church where I met the girl I would eventually marry. My two older sisters married young men from this congregation. Adolescence, puberty, and youth group activities were themes of that era. The youth group would come to our farm for hayrides and bonfires. At dusk, during one of those gatherings, I stuffed some of my clothes with straw, climbed to the top of the silo, let out a shriek, and tossed the dummy from the top of the silo into the group gathered below. My mother was unhappy with me for that prank.

Eventually, my parents drifted apart and separated. My mother moved to town with my younger sister and me. Dad had a farm sale, quit farming, and took a welding job with Caterpillar Tractor. I stopped attending church and school. Cars, girls, working, and playing pool occupied me. I enlisted in the U.S. Army.

I am a U.S. Army Vietnam veteran. I served in Vietnam from 1969 to 1971, stationed at the edge of Saigon, where I assisted the military in offloading cargo ships at the Saigon seaport and transporting supplies to outlying units. When I was there, the city, built for a million people, was bulging with three million people, many of them refugees from the war.

One day in Saigon in 1969, I was walking along a city street when I noticed a group of children playing together. They were probably five to ten years old. I looked their way and smiled, and they responded with smiles and laughter, moving toward me. I anticipated they would ask for money. They gathered around, and I interpreted the encounter as a friendly meeting between young children and an American soldier until I realized that every one of the children had a hand in one of the pockets of my jungle fatigues! I twisted and turned, and then jumped away from the group. As I got several yards away, I looked back and noticed one little guy standing with his hand to his head, crying. In my twisting and turning, my elbow had bumped the side of his head and had hurt him.

The children I encountered on that street in Saigon were part of a refugee population trying to survive in any way they could. Several years after my military service, I reflected on my encounter with the city's street children. I wondered what I had been doing in a situation where I was harming a child, a child who was put into the position of trying to survive on the streets of Saigon because of the actions of my government and its military. I began to think about the mission I had participated in as a soldier.

My encounter in Saigon was benign compared to the horrors experienced by the children, families, and soldiers of Vietnam as bombs and bullets tore into their flesh and land, killing and maiming precious lives created in God's image and creating wounds and scars that would last for generations. As I reflected on the impact of war and learned more about what was happening to the people involved, I came to realize that these stories are repeated in every place and every time there is war and violence. Everyone suffers, especially the innocent, especially the children. I became aware of the consequences of conflict and violence taking place in the world and their impact on real people. I learned that nations' vast resources are poured into weaponry, armaments, and military personnel. Vast resources are taken away from the hungry, the poor, the sick, and the oppressed.

Two

I Called It Swimming

By Ted Huffman

I called it swimming. Floating would be a more accurate description. I waded into the river, adjusting to the cold water until I was deep enough to be swept off my feet. I knew not to be afraid of the river. I turned downstream and allowed the river to carry me, avoiding the big rocks by seeking the path of the deepest flow. I could hold my head above the surface to breathe, but I wanted to look underwater, too. As a kid who had worn glasses for years and still experienced the world slightly out of focus, I appreciated the clarity of vision through the water. I knew where the big lunker trout swam, facing upstream. I knew where the water calmed and grew shallow enough to get out, and, shivering, I gained the shore to walk back upstream. I knew that river. I loved that river.

My childhood is awash in memories of being immersed in water, but I don't remember my baptism into the Christian church. Yet, I do not doubt it happened. I have seen a photograph of me, my parents, a friend who was born 20 days before me, his parents, and the minister in a black robe. I have a certificate signed by Rev. E. Brentwood Barker, and my baptism is recorded in the records of my home church. Though she is not in the picture, my sister was there. She was two years old and doesn't remember the words that were said. I know, however, that Rev. Barker spoke the words of our tradition about rising into new life from the water of baptism.

I remember the river flowing between the cottonwood trees high in the mountains. I remember the river as the place of my baptism. In the river, I learned the sacredness of my birthplace and the strength of the love and values my family gave me. I love the river. Just as the river changed, so did I.

I grew up and moved away from the river and the state of my birth. I put miles between myself and my hometown people and my growing-up years.

In college and seminary, I wrestled with the sacred texts of our people. One of the stories of Jesus that frequently comes up is from the third chapter of John's Gospel. It reports a nighttime conversation between Jesus and Nicodemus. They engage in some verbal sparring about humans in God's realm. Nicodemus questions Jesus about being born again. Jesus answers that being born of water and Spirit is the way to enter God's realm. In my student days, the rise of Evangelical and non-denominational groups such as Campus Crusade for Christ was powered by slogans such as "One Way" and "Are You Born Again?" I found most of those evangelical approaches to be intellectually unsatisfying and disconnected from the stark realities of the Civil Rights Movement, the War in Vietnam, and other critical political and moral issues of the time. I experienced Jesus' teaching as directly relevant to the day's ethical issues. I was offended by the idea of focusing on personal salvation without considering the suffering caused by injustice.

Later, as a working preacher, I struggled with Nicodemus's question: "How can anyone be born after having grown old?" I studied the text, preached, and taught classes. But ultimately, it was not an academic study or late-night conversations that widened my understanding. What changed was a real-life experience that occurred when I was over 65 years old.

I might call it swimming. Floating would be a more accurate description. Suddenly, I was over my head and swept along by a current mightier than any I had experienced. I was not in a river but in a hospital. Like the river, the hospital was a familiar place. As a chaplain, I had been granted access to the entire institution and had visited most of the treatment areas. I had been to the emergency room in the middle of the night. I knew that there were small consultation rooms that I could access to counsel those whose lives were disrupted by trauma and grief. I understood the protocols of washing, gowning, gloving, and putting on a face mask. I was granted access to places with restricted entry. I knew what each of the codes called on the PA system was.

That day, I arrived at the hospital early. It was a busy day in a busy week. Two days prior, I had officiated at two funerals, one of which was a huge gathering for a fallen firefighter who left behind a young widow and two preschool daughters. His sudden and traumatic death had shocked the community, and I had put in long hours choosing my words carefully. The next day, I led worship in our congregation and spoke openly and directly about mental illness and death by suicide. Before arriving at the hospital, I had showered and dressed in a suit because I had another funeral scheduled for that morning. I also had plans to meet with yet another family planning a funeral for a loved one. With my wife and colleague in the hospital, I struggled to balance my duties.

I entered the hospital through a side entrance, using my ID badge to gain access to an employee's area. I climbed the stairs to the sixth floor, mindful of my tendency to overeat and exercise too little, especially during times of stress. In my suit and tie, I greeted my wife, colleague, and life partner with a kiss and took a seat in a chair next to the bed. We chatted a bit. She drifted to sleep, and I took a moment for private prayer.

Suddenly, I heard the call over the PA: "Rapid Response, Rapid Response!" I barely recognized that they were calling the room I was in before the crash cart and response team rushed in. I moved away from the bed to give them room to work and stood next to the window when I heard, "Code Blue, Code Blue, Room!" My prayers became desperate, and I had no words except "Help!"

CPR is incredibly violent. I knew that. I was CPR certified. I had previously performed CPR on a heart attack victim for ten minutes while we waited for EMTs to arrive. But it seemed doubly violent when the body in the bed was my wife of 46 years.

I might call it swimming. Floating would be a more accurate description. I was desperately trying to keep my head above water. I worried that I might faint, and I desperately did not want to do anything that might distract responders from their work with my wife. When I finally heard a nurse at her feet call, I had a pulse; I must have been holding my breath because I let out a burst of air. The subsequent deep inhale refreshed me, and the light-headedness faded, but I was swimming in brain fog.

As they wheeled her out of the room, I knew they were headed to the Intensive Care Unit one floor below. I knew that my ID would grant me access, but I also knew that I had to use elevators different from the large ones reserved for gurneys. I felt panic creep in. I couldn't remember where the passenger elevators were. I tried to imagine the tower's floor plan, where we were located, and the locations of stairs and elevators, but I was confused. I worried that I might not be able to find her.

Fortunately, the hospital had experience with disoriented family members. I should have remembered. I had been assigned to that duty many times. An aide was assigned to escort me to the ICU waiting room and stay with me while the doctors did their work. Gradually, I recovered my focus. I started to tell the aide that my wife's cardiologist should be in the consultation room next to the ICU because he was bringing a new electrophysiologist to consider other options for solving Susan's arrhythmia when I heard the call for another code blue in the ICU.

I was swimming again. I was in over my head. I didn't know what to do. I knew that I needed to stay out of the treatment area so that all its resources could be focused on caring for her. I tried to be patient, pray, and wait. When I came up for air, I asked the aide to walk into the ICU and check to see if she was still alive. After what seemed like a very long time, but probably was just a few minutes, she returned with the news that she was in a room where they were adjusting some medications and doing a bit of cleanup, and that I could go in to visit her sometime within an hour.

Waiting isn't my long suit. To stay afloat, I needed to be doing. I called our licensed pastor and asked her to cover the morning's funeral for me. I had a complete manuscript of the service printed and on the table in my office. She had to take time off from her day job, but she quickly made the arrangements to be away from work. The next task that came to my mind was to call our children, but I wasn't ready to do that yet. I needed to see Susan and assess the situation. I had spent enough time

in the hospital with patients in critical condition
to know that brain damage was a distinct possibility after multiple cardiac arrests. I didn't want to
think about that. I called my friend and colleague,
a pastor at an Evangelical Lutheran Church in our
community. I asked him if he could cover the funeral I was scheduled to officiate in a few days. I
told him I had never missed a funeral as a pastor,
and now I was missing two in the same week.

Fifteen minutes after I called, my friend offered
a prayer at my side in the waiting room. I went
swimming in my tears. I thought of myself as
someone calm in a crisis, but I felt like I might col-
lapse at any moment. He reminded me of something I had told others and had mentioned to him
many times. "When you have no words for your
prayers, it is good to remember that you aren't the
only one praying." He reminded me that our licensed minister would have already activated our
prayer chain, and he had done the same in his
church.

Finally, I was allowed to go into the ICU and
see Susan. In a couple of hours, we had gone from
having a conversation to her being in the ICU on

a ventilator with a port in her upper chest with nine different IV pumps plumbed into it. One of the medicines was fentanyl. Just reading its name on the pump was enough to make me afraid. I was swimming. A nurse informed me that the medication would make her sleep. I was told the ventilator was temporary to give her system a chance to rest and recover, that her heart had slowed to a regular rate, and that she was stable.

In over my head, I wasn't sure what to do next. I called our son and Susan's sisters to tell them what had happened. I asked them not to call our daughter, as I hadn't called her yet. I was waiting for two things and planning to call her later. She was living in Japan, and I wanted to call her during the day. I also wanted to have our Lay Minister at my side so she could take over the call if I was unable to control my emotions and got to sobbing.

The nursing staff at the ICU changed at 11 pm. By that time, a lot had changed. Our son was on his way, flying in from Washington. Our licensed minister would pick him up at the airport and take him to the hospital, where he could use my car to sleep at our house. Susan's youngest sister had flown from Oregon to Montana, where my sister picked her up at the airport, and they were on the road to South Dakota. Susan had been awake. She couldn't talk, but she wrote me a few notes. She wrote that she didn't need people to come because she would be OK, that the beds at home all had clean sheets, and that she loved me. A nurse whose name I did not yet know brought me a warm blanket and suggested that I take off my tie. I had forgotten I was dressed in a suit and tie for a funeral.

I sat by her side all night long, holding her hand, offering a sliver of ice from time to time, and praying for a happy ending. I was swimming—floating on top of a flood of dreams, memories, and hopes. I thought of our first date fifty years earlier, when I was sixteen. I thought I didn't know how to be an adult without her. I realized that I would pay any price and do anything I could for one more conversation, one more day.

I have visited the ICU many times. I had sat with families as they worried about their loved ones. I had prayed with individuals as their spouses died. I had officiated at funerals. I knew all the protocols and most of the nurses and doctors. I had never been immersed in the ICU from the inside. I was in over my head. I was too tired to sleep. I was too exhausted to think rationally. I floated between dreams, waking with a start and a panic every time the hospital PA sounded. During the night, I heard the call for another code blue. I heard the gentle chimes played when a baby was born in the delivery center. I listened to the muted conversations at the nursing station. The nurses kept offering me tea, coffee, and water. I didn't want those things. What I wanted was something that they could not promise.

Years have passed since that night. Susan slowly recovered. The electrophysiologist who met her by performing CPR performed a cryoablation that corrected the arrhythmia. We retired and moved. I developed atrial flutter and had my ablation procedure. We have walked together nearly every day since she recovered.

I understand what Nicodemus could not. I know what evangelicals might not, with their "born again" theology. I emerged from swimming in the critical care unit as born again as I can imagine. Unlike my first baptism, I will remember this one, and I will never cease to be grateful for what happened.

I once thought my story began with my birth. My mother walked to the hospital, and I arrived before the doctor. I was the first boy after three girls. Our house had become so small and cramped that an addition was soon under construction. I grew up surrounded by love. However, I have discovered more than one beginning to my story. I emerged from my wife's experience and was born again. This is now where my story begins.

Three

I'm Good At What I Do

By Ike Porter

A veteran asked to see me as his outpatient therapist, and his treatment team agreed to this. It was unusual, yet I had the degrees and experience necessary to support the decision. Zeke became one of my outpatients.

Zeke graduated from the Naval Academy and had played 4 seasons for Navy football. He had been assigned to the procurement office on a major battleship in the U.S. Navy. He was tasked with procuring computers for the senior staff on the ship. He found a fantastic deal, but it was too expensive for his budget, so he borrowed funds from another line item on the ship without clearing the action with his superior officers. He justified this in his mind and envisioned the commendations he would receive.

Unfortunately for him, the Navy did not see it his way and sought to court-martial him and give him a dishonorable discharge. The personal chaos around this caused Zeke to have a complete psychotic break. He was eventually diagnosed as bipolar with psychotic features. Zeke's father was a man of influence, and he hired a very capable lawyer. After intense negotiations, the matter was resolved, with Zeke being medically discharged from the U.S. Navy at his current rank. (This is incredibly important. Had Zeke received a dishonorable discharge, he would not have been eligible for any benefits from the Department of Veterans Affairs (VA).) As it stood, Zeke was 100% Service-Connected, which is currently $ 50,416 per year (tax-free) with a spouse. The amount would increase with additional dependents. Understand that the money is tax-free, and the VA takes care of the veteran's health care, including vision and dental care, for the veteran and their family. There is also college assistance for their children. Had Zeke been dishonorably discharged, this would not have been available to him, and I would never have met him.

Zeke was seeing me for an hour every two weeks. His progress was consistent in his appearance at appointments. He had two behaviors that I sought to address with him. One was his obsession with a woman who had broken their engagement when Zeke had his breakdown. The other was his consistent pattern of talking the doctors into reducing his medication until it was below therapeutic levels. When Zeke started missing appointments, I knew he had succeeded in getting his meds reduced.

Over the years, I met Zeke's father, brother, and sister-in-law. They felt free to call me and tell me what they knew. I was unable to report to them due to HIPAA regulations. However, on a couple of occasions, they would be in my office with Zeke, and I would talk about Zeke's illness and his progress only with Zeke's permission.

On one occasion, Zeke started missing appointments, and I discovered that he had also missed his appointment for his medication. A few months later, I was in my garage on a hot and muggy Saturday afternoon, and my VA cell phone rang. I answered it, and it was Zeke. "Hey, Chaplain Ike. Guess where I am. "

"Zeke, I haven't seen you for some weeks. Where are you?"

Zeke responds with, "I'm on the football field of Texas A&M, trying out for the team." (I knew that Zeke was out of shape and hadn't been working out at all. He had put on several pounds around his waist.)

I replied, "Zeke, this raises many questions for me. You're in your 40s and are competing with 18 to 25-year-olds. I think you've probably lost a step or two. What do you think?"

Zeke says, "But I've got the experience, I'll make these guys look like 2-year-olds."

I said, "Zeke, I think you're setting yourself up for disappointment. I don't want that to happen to you. Why don't you come back to Battle Creek, where we can talk?"

He responds with, "I'm gonna go on the field and show them how it's done."

I say, "Okay, Zeke, if you don't make it, return to where you are loved."

Zeke says, "Okay, Chaplain Ike. I appreciate all that you have done for me."

I've pieced together that Zeke failed to get on Texas A&M's football team, so he began the long and arduous drive from Texas to Michigan. On the way, he stopped at his home of origin, and while there, he threatened one of his high school classmates who was now a police detective. Zeke was looking for his fiancée, who had married someone else many years ago. He created such an overall sense of fear that he was arrested and convicted. He spent 13 months in a prison psych ward. Zeke later reported that the experience was not a good one for him. He returned to our facility as a psych transfer. Almost as soon as he arrived, he requested a visit from me (something his father had requested before Zeke got to the Battle Creek facility.) I went to see Zeke at my first opportunity. He was somewhat subdued when I saw him. We hugged briefly. His illness had put him through his own hell. I found myself being angry at the mental health physicians who allowed themselves to be talked down about the amount of medication. Zeke's physicians didn't accept any responsibility, even though it was their action that led to Zeke's going below therapeutic dosage and ending up in prison.

Zeke and I resumed our once-every-two-week appointments. He agreed that his ex-girlfriend had a right to her own life. Sometimes he would still obsess and try to figure out how many times a male's appendage had entered his ex-girlfriend. Of course, I discouraged this type of obsession and worked on developing redirecting techniques Zeke could use.

Zeke definitely changed during his time in prison. He was frightened by the police now. Things were going pretty well until Zeke stopped coming to my office again. He had once again talked the physicians into reducing his medications. (The first thing Zeke did when he got off his medications was to have his phone number changed and unlisted.) Mental illness doesn't mean mental stupidity.

I was going along with my life when I received a call from Zeke's brother. Zeke had called his brother's wife and asked her how she would like to raise her children as a single parent. Zeke had threatened his brother on more than one occasion, so he was taking this threat seriously. He managed to *69 his brother's number, and he sent it to me via e-mail. I called the number right away and didn't get an answer so I left a message for Zeke to call me when he could. That afternoon, on my way home, my phone rang, and it was Zeke. I pulled the car over and talked with Zeke.

Me: Hello

Zeke: Chaplain Ike?

Me: Yes, is this Zeke?

Zeke: Yes, how did you get my number?

Me: "Zeke, why don't you come in? We can talk about this and get you back on your medication." (All the time I am racking my brain. I cannot tell him that his brother, whose life Zeke had just threatened, had given me the phone number.)

Zeke: (In a demanding voice) How did you get my number?

Me: The only thing I could think of was to say, "God gave it to me."

Zeke: "Why to hell would God give you my phone number?"

Me: "I don't know, Zeke. Maybe it's because I'm good at what I do. At any rate, I think it would be best for you to come into the hospital and get checked out."

Zeke, "Don't call me again!"

The next day, I was sitting at my desk when I heard a pounding on my office door. I almost jumped out of my skin, but I didn't have to wait long. Zeke came into my office without waiting for me to invite him in.

I said, "Good Morning, Zeke, (I nodded toward a chair in front of my desk) have a seat." Zeke shot around my desk and came at me. I had been trained in Non-Abusive Psychological and Physical Intervention (NAPPI), but all I had time for was to push my chair away from my desk and into the corner. I had crossed my arms in front of my chest to raise them up to protect my face or lower them to protect my stomach and groin areas. Zeke planted his leg up against my chair between my legs. My phones were out of reach. I sat there knowing I was going to get hurt. As has been said,

Zeke had been a lineman for the Navy Football team—he was not a small man.

I was in my chair with my face tilted up, looking up at this man, trying to remember that I am a pacifist Christian, and wondering how I was going to escape. I had run scenarios through my mind. I could hit him in the groin, but that would leave my face open for attack. I could hit him in the face, but that would leave my stomach and groin open for his knee attack. There was no option for physical intervention.

Finally, a statement came to mind, "Please go to the other side of my desk, I'm feeling very threatened right now."

Zeke asked, "What did you say?"

I replied, "Please go to the other side of my desk, I'm feeling very threatened right now."

Zeke just grinned at me, and it dawned on me that he was enjoying this.

So I said again, "Please go to the other side of my desk, I'm feeling very threatened right now."

He continued to grin and said in a dark voice. "I'm good at what I do."

I thought, *"He's using my words against me."* So, again, I said, "Please go to the other side of my desk. I'm feeling very threatened right now."

He replied, "I'm good at what I do. I'm good at what I do."

Looking up at him, I said, "Yes, you are good at what you do. Now, please go to the other side of my desk, and I'm feeling very threatened right now."

Zeke backed away from me and went toward the door. I immediately went to my phone and dialed the police. The police station was next door to my building.

Ten minutes later, the police called me and said, "We have apprehended Mr. Zeke. Do you want to press charges?"

I was surprised that the VA police suggested pressing charges. I responded, "No, I want him committed. He is ill."

So, Zeke was taken to the admitting team. They decided that he was mentally ill and needed to be committed because Zeke told them, "Chaplain Porter said that God gave him my phone number."

I read this in Zeke's chart and began wrestling with whether I should lie or not. What if, when I got on the stand, I was asked if I had told Zeke that God had given me his phone number? If I lied and said I didn't, I would lose all credibility with Zeke; I would probably be committed if I admitted to saying it without the back story. About a week later, I had to go to court. We had a courtroom right there on the hospital campus. Zeke had dismissed his attorney and decided to represent himself. Much of what he said in the courtroom revealed his illness, and the judge committed him. I didn't have to give any testimony. Was God protecting me from myself?

I had what I considered a brilliant insight. When Zeke got off his meds, in his mind, he reverted to the age when he had his first mental break. He had a right to chase after his girlfriend, he had a right to threaten his brother, he had a right to threaten his high school buddy, and he could play football. Every time he got off his medication, he was a 22-year-old guy again.

Zeke and I continued to meet until he met an age-appropriate woman who understood his illness. She was a pharmacist. Zeke moved in with her in a city that was some distance away. He would come in for a visit every couple of months. On one occasion, he asked if I would do his wedding. I told him yes if both he and his fiancée wanted me to.

Unfortunately, Zeke stopped taking his meds again, and this caused a great deal of confusion for his fiancée, and the wedding was put on hold. I saw Zeke one more time after that. He was resigned to taking his medications. He was living with his fiancée. He expressed deep gratitude that I was there for him. His father and mother had died, and his siblings would not/could not reconcile. So, Zeke's family became other veterans and his fiancée. Before I wrote this, I learned of Zeke's death. He never married, and he had no children. I am saddened that Zeke is no longer here.

Four

The Accident and Tezeta

By Anne King-Grosh

I'm nearly at the bridge. Just another couple of miles and I will be home. On this drive home, I've thought back on the week, and my decision has been made. I will find a way to say what I have finally decided to say even though it's going to be hard. Suddenly, car lights are coming fast and shining into my eyes. I have been hit, smashed head-on. Mercifully, there is no memory of the noise of metal against metal, of the skidding screech of tires, of the sudden hard jolt to a stop. I wiggle my toes of my right foot. Am I paralyzed? It's my greatest fear. No, I am not. A deep howl is rising up through me, and then, I feel an arm around my shoulders. "You're okay," says a voice, "You're going to be okay". I know I am not okay, but his voice is soothing and I hang onto it. He creates a safe place. "You're okay. You'll be okay."

In the emergency room, I beg the nurse not to cut my jeans off. I think, "I have to call the hospital and tell them I won't be in tomorrow". I take my contacts out. And then, I wake up and there's a tube in my throat. I can't get it out. It hurts, and I try to pull it and bite on it so that it stops rubbing against my throat. I float back down into a dark abyss and then up again. I can't breathe. I'm fighting to breathe, trying to get that tube out of my throat and grabbing at it. Hands take mine and tie them down. A disembodied voice yells, "Get the trach set". Back down into that dark abyss I go again.

I'm on a hospital bed, covered only with a sheet next to my naked body. I'm so, so cold. I can't stop shaking from the cold. I beg for blankets. I can't have blankets. My body is too hot. I can't curl up to stay warm. My leg is in traction, and the weight is heavy. My back hurts, I can't turn over. Tubes carry fluid into my body and then back out. I feel like I am going mad! Dad rubs my feet, says little, but the touch grounds me, creates a safe spot for my mind to rest.

Later, another surgery. Narcotics to dull the pain that feels like it will kill me. Visitors pray for me. They visit me. I wish some would leave sooner. They make me tired by their presence. Others calm me. I feel loved and cared for. Week after week, they come and go while I stay on my back in bed. I have a thought. I visualize Jesus sitting on a chair right inside of my hospital room. Jesus chooses to stay in my room, a witness to my immobility. Such a comfort!

I left the hospital 5 weeks and 2 surgeries after the accident. I put all my energy into the PT sessions that ever so slowly tore the adhesion that grew in my knee after my knee cap was wired together. I was determined to be able to bend my knee and walk normally again. Six months of rehab and I was back to work. All these years, I have carried the image of Jesus sitting by the door of my hospital room; Jesus chooses to stay, is not afraid of my pain.

Can I stay with those in pain when I can not fix life for them? Little did I know how this "vision" of Jesus staying with me would carry me through the succeeding decades of my life.

Ufaessa's little 3 yr. old girl has been sick for such a long time. He has taken her to this doctor and that doctor and no one seems to be able to really help her. She got Griseofulvin for some skin problems even though I couldn't see any place where she really had a skin problem. I gave her high-protein food over the last weeks because she had so much edema, it looked like she had Kwashiorkor, but that wasn't her only problem either. She has been exposed to TB for some length of time but her x-rays were read to be normal except for some pneumonia. She certainly has more than pneumonia! I think she has TB and HIV. She has been so weak, a little three-year-old who can't stand or walk a lot of the time. She has mucous that is very tenacious and rattles her lungs with every breath. She has taken this antibiotic and that antibiotic. Ufaessa has talked about her dying. He is weary from the pain of her being sick and hearing her cry every time she gets one more injection or one more blood specimen. She is weary too. He took her one day to a healing service and afterwards had a vision of her running and playing, completely well. While he saw her like this, he felt a strong flood of well-being, like a gush of water, pour over him and wash around Tezeta. He felt she was healed. And she did play and seem better for a short amount of time, but then she was back the way she was before. "I think", he says, "I saw a vision of how she would be healed when she goes to heaven. I think she is going to die, and that is okay".

Last night, Fanti, Ufaessa's wife, called me to their tiny one-room house. Our family has been to their home many times for *injera and wat*, the traditional food of Ethiopia. Fanti's *what* is red pepper hot, so hot that I need to drink some Coke between bites. Her *buna* is flavored coffee before flavored coffee was sold in the stores. She roasts her beans with whole cloves, pounds the two together and serves it to us with two small spoons of sugar.

Fanti could be said to be "dirt poor" but I find her abundantly rich in hospitality!

This home is the only size they can afford. They live here with their 3 children. Fanti is a strong woman. Two years ago when I learned to know her, she told me about running away from home. "My father was going to make me marry this older man and I had no intentions to marry him. But what could I do? I was only 13 years old. So, a few days before the wedding, I left our house in the dark of the night and went as far from home as I was brave enough to go in the darkness. And then I climbed an acacia tree and hid myself in its branches. My parents couldn't find me. I stayed there for the day until it was dark again and then walked some more. I never went home again and never saw my parents again". Fanti is a strong woman.

But now, Fanti's strength is of no use to heal her daughter. She and her landlord lady are very concerned about how weak Tezeta is. She hasn't drunk anything for a day and has only urinated once. Tezeta looks miserable, a little girl who should be up and running around, but instead can not hold up her own head for any length of time. Her left arm is almost functionless as it has been for some time. She keeps calling her mother and saying, "I'm sick, I'm sick." She complains that her stomach hurts, though it is nice and soft and doesn't seem tender when I palpate it. In the past, I have tried to decide if I should try to take her to one more place and see if we can't find out what is wrong with her. But I don't know where else we can go. Ethiopia is in a war that eats up everything: Health care, food, infrastructure, and trust in the government. The health system is a mess. Even I, a white nurse, have no confidence in the local clinics or the hospitals.

Tonight it feels like this is it for her and we should let her die in peace. I offer to take her to the hospital if Fanti wants me to. She finds it hard to decide, especially as Ufaessa isn't here. He was in prison more than a day's travel away because a relative for whom he promised to be guarantor stole some stuff and ran. Now that he has been released from prison, he can bring the relative, who has been found, back from another city to the prison here in Addis Ababa. So, Fanti is here alone with the three children. Tiruwerkna, the landlady, advised her not to take her to the hospital. And I think this is probably the best advice. The hospital would probably give her some glucose that might help for a short time but in the long run wouldn't help her. But, I tell Fanti, we could go and try anyway. She decides we won't go, though she never says so directly to me.

I suggest that Fanti make Tezeta some tea and I tell Fanti that we will see if she can drink that with a syringe. I lace the tea with plenty of sugar, and sure enough, she opens her mouth and swallows it when I push the tea in with the syringe. This seems to encourage both of the women, and they drink their tea too while I feed Tezeta. Three other Christian believers came and brought a sweater that they had taken to the Finnish mission church, where they had prayed for Tezeta. "Take this sweater", they tell Fanti, "and wrap it around her. Have faith that it will heal her." My prayer with them earlier in the day was a prayer for peace to abound in this beloved home. I felt Tezeta was soon going to die.

I left their home at about 8:30 in the evening. The next morning I get up feeling Tezeta has died. And that is the message I got. I went to the house and there, on a white plastic grain sack stuffed with dried grass to make it a seat, sits Fanti rocking back and forth in front of the only bed they have. On it lies Tezeta, covered up in a white homespun cotton *gabardine,* the cloth that is a blanket, a coat, or in this case, a shroud. I kneel beside Fanti in silence with my arm wrapped around her, one mother to another. I stay beside her for a time and then move back to let her sit there alone, as all the other women who have already gathered are also doing. Soon, Fanti begins to cry out short words - "*Imyae, imyae, hode, hode*". "Mommy, mommy, my stomach, my stomach." While we sit there, a man comes with a string and measures Tezeta's body so that they can buy an appropriately sized box. I stay for a short while and then walk the few hundred meters back to my own home to help our 3 children get their breakfast. In 45 minutes or so I return to the house with Yeshi, our secretary. More people have gathered and are all sitting in silence while Fanti rocks herself in front of the bed. This time she cries out her hard questions to God: "Why didn't she wait until her father comes home? I have left all my family to follow you, why have you shamed me so?" The lady who has brought the sweater the night before comes and immediately tells me that they hadn't known this is God's plan for Tezeta and so she has died despite the prayer and faith for her healing. I understand her but I don't understand. While we sit together, the measuring man returns with a very small, plain little box for Tezeta's body. I return home.

Pastor Mateous from the church down the dirt road comes to talk to us about the funeral arrangements. Our community is a poor enclave on the edge of the capital city, Addis Ababa. Many of our neighbors have been treated for leprosy or work at the leprosy research hospital that is close by. Leprosy creates a marginalizing identity in our neighborhood. "Why would you buy injera in your neighborhood?" asks a well-educated Ethiopian friend of ours. "You know, you could get leprosy from eating that injera!"

Because Tezeta's family hasn't had enough money to join an *ider. (*An ider is a group of people who organize themselves to act as death and support insurance for each other. Each family pays about $.50 or more each month and is obligated to help organize the funerals of any members of the ider and help prepare food for the mourners after the funeral and for the next several days) they have to rely on the local church that they attend to carry out the funeral for them. The problem is that the local church has so many very poor members that they have no more money left in their fund for the funeral. We give Pastor Mateous money for the box, for the food for the mourners, and for digging the hole for the box. As we are talking, he tells us this story:

> "I have so many very poor people come into my office asking for money, food, whatever. Sometimes I am sooo tired and I don't know how I can keep going. I ask God why I shouldn't go and pastor somewhere else. But he has called me here, so as long as he gives me the strength, I will keep working here in this neighborhood. Several days ago a man came to me who

had nothing. His wife had died. He has a small child, about a year old, and is currently unemployed. 'I can work', he told me. 'I'm strong. I can do any heavy work. But there is no work. How can I take care of my child?' Seeing how distressed this man was, I took 10 birr *from my salary* and gave it to the man. "I will give you 10 *birr* every month to take care of your child, I told him. However, I have something even better than that that will bring you comfort. It won't make your troubles any less, and it might even make them worse, but you will have comfort. I told him about Jesus and he became a believer. He came to church last Sunday and was very happy."

Later in the morning, we visit Fanti's house, and Mateious gives a short talk about our real life in Jesus and our eternal presence with Him. We then take Fanti and her three children, as well as those accompanying her, in the three Mennonite Mission vehicles parked at our office, and drive 20 minutes to the cemetery, where we hold a brief meditation by the grave. Fanti has a hard time. She beats her chest over and over until one of the women takes her arm and restrains her. The Christian believers with her are afraid that her loud, traditional way of mourning will spoil their witness. It's important to them to show a distinction between themselves and the Christian Orthodox who might be among them. (Tezeta needed to be buried at this cemetery rather than just up the hill behind our house at the Orthodox church cemetery because her parents are "believers" and the Orthodox priests will not allow believers to be buried in their cemeteries).

We are at the cemetery a short time and than come back to Fanti's house and sit together to eat and drink coffee.

Sunday, 2 days after the funeral, I went back to the house and sat with the family. I was urged to sit on the mattress with the women, the traditional way for the women of the extended family to mourn. This felt especially sacred to me because I knew I was invited to be one of them. Ufaessa had returned home by this time. And as there was no way for anyone to get the message to him, he had no idea that his daughter had died. Without embalming, the funeral had to be carried out the day Tezeta died. We drank coffee and ate kolo, a grain snack. We visited together and chatted.

Our friends were poor in riches but rich in community.

Five

Brother Baby James
Air

By Marc Stewart

The night of brother James' birth must be my earliest memory. Sometimes, I wonder if it will make it into an episode of "Call the Midwife" set in London in the early '60s. For now, it replays like a treasured Super 8 home movie with every care given to protect the yellowed celluloid film. It's so sweet to see. It is delicate, and I want everything to be just right so that it doesn't get broken. I don't have a fine silver screen on which to project it. That's okay. My focus is not so sharp. Nothing is lost by projecting it on what has become the crinkly home screen of my life. So, I rest into the leather armchair in my corner of the living room with my snack bag of soft salted, butterscotch caramels. I unwrap a caramel to chew on as the projector clicks through the opening credit lines of a sweet, salty story. There's older brother Dana, Nana Longwell, Mom and Dad, and baby James, and an onsite location credit to 72 Kingswood Avenue, Beckenham, Kent, England, and the Congregational Church in Shortlands with a memorial attribution to Reverend Cyril Peat (d. 1962). Time for another caramel.

Dana and I had been allowed a longer evening play time than usual, an hour more than our 7 pm bedtime. It was extra-super special. We got to be in the downstairs parlor, and Nana Longwell was with us. Nana had flown all the way over from the United States to visit. Dana and I felt like cowboy "pardners" all dressed up in the blue jeans and flannel shirts she had brought for us. We were quite a sight in that proper English parlor. That night, Nana was teaching us her favorite American Cowboy song. "Oh, give me a home where the buffalo roam," we howled.

Knuckles rapped on the parlor door. Nana Longwell shushed us and told us not to let out a peep. As she opened the door to slip out, we heard crying that we had never heard before. Dana and I dared not utter a thing. She turned and whispered, "I'll be back." Our eyes, already wide open to the soft parlor light, opened wider with wonder. Or, was it fright? We could only stare at each other. No sound was heard, even as Nana returned and opened the parlor door wide. Our eyes turned to pierce her, looking for what was happening.

Before either of us could blurt out a word or a cry of fright, Nana looked so tenderly back into our eyes and whispered, "Shhh, you have a new baby brother." Nana led us up the staircase. Behind the closed door at the end of the hallway were our mother, father, and newborn brother, James.

I can still hear my lilt in my English lad accent floating through the night. "Nana, can we see the baby?"

Nana's Worcester, Massachusetts, Yankee voice was pointed. "No, to your room, you two, it's long past bedtime."

Our faint shadows glided along the maroon-velveted wallpaper. That hallway wallpaper softened so much about our home. Harsh voices did not rise so sharply up the staircase. Neither did our gleeful yelps echo around the house. The raised velvet gave a 3-D effect, like the hall was alive. It made our shadows dance, but it could not be touched. We knew, without a doubt, to keep our "dirty fingers off." Still, Nana felt its softness, along with a gentle touch, taking our hands.

Nana promised, "You'll get to see your baby brother James in the morning." She tucked us. "Sweet dreams."

Dana and I awakened to a bright Friday morning. Summer was arriving within a few weeks. A streak of light piercing through the curtain's edge seemed to promise it would be a good day. Pulling aside the curtains, I could see colorful gardens all the way up Kingsbury Avenue. Nana came in to help us dress and put on some play clothes. Then, I remembered baby James. Nana already figured out a plan: "First, we're going to have breakfast and then you can go out to play for a while. James and your mom are still sleeping. You will get to see James after he wakes up. And do you know? It is also your mother's birthday today!"

Dana and I burst out into the beauty of lush English gardens. Dana is on his scooter, and I am on my trike. All caution to the wind, we had a world to explore. We rolled out the front driveway and headed up the sidewalk towards Marco's home. There were only 10 houses up the corner where Marco lived. Marco was a friend, and we enjoyed the play on our names, Marc and Marco. We laughed when he said we had the same name except for an "o" because he was from Italy. I was excited to tell Marco that we had a new brother and to ask him how to say "James" in Italy.

What might the neighbors think to see this giddy 3-year-old toddler and his determined 6-year-old brother? Like ladybugs fluttering in a flower garden, our attention turned to the beauty all around us. Everything looked "all things bright and beautiful," just like what we sang in Sunday School. Each home on the avenue wore a piece of

Eden, with flower gardens lining the sidewalk. My favorites were the snap dragons. I felt like a dragon tamer when I squeezed the flower, like making dragon jaws open wide and ready to swallow any bug that dares come flying by. There were yellow and white snap dragons, and some pink and red, and purple. I gleefully picked as many as I could. Some even came out by the roots. I stuffed them all into the boot of my tricycle. It was filled before we even made it halfway to Marco's. We sped home so I could color the dining room table with dozens of snap dragons. I'd make our home look like the center of the world that it was.

This would be a time for another caramel. I'm so engaged in the memory playing out. I distract myself with the flashing realization of why movie theater snack stand candy is boxed and not wrapped. The crackling of the cellophane briefly interrupts the sweet scene.

If I had imagined myself to be a dragon tamer or an agile ladybug, our morning bustle was not so pretty. The neighbors were angry. Ladybugs working a garden do not leave gaping holes in the soil where there used to be flowers. And, the dining room might not have felt itself duly adorned. Most of the flowers I had pulled were crushed. As I set them out on the dining room table, clumps of dirt spilled out of the roots. It wasn't quite what I imagined it could look like, but it was my contribution to the day. Dragon tamers do not flinch from making the world great.

Nana promptly sent us both to the bathroom to strip down, jump in the tub, and soak. She had to keep going out to answer phone calls from neighbors. I heard Nana trying to spread the good cheer of our floral efforts as she answered the phone: "Harriet Longwell, here, at the Stewarts' home, how are you this beautiful English morning?"

God loves Nana; she must have been trying to start out with the best, most positive words she could think of. How she would have wanted to continue straight into blurting out that her youngest daughter just had a baby last night, and everyone was doing wonderfully. But that was not the English etiquette in this reserved and highly formal neighborhood. People answered their phones by only stating their phone numbers and not sharing anything as personal as their names. And we can be sure, here, that as soon as the caller was assured that it was the Stewart home, they would have berated Nana for the mess her grand-children made of their flower beds. After each call, Nana returned and asked how many flowers we had taken from that neighbor's garden.

As the muddied bath water cooled, Dad burst in and demanded to know what we thought we were doing. Not even the velvet wallpaper in the hallway would have muffled my cries of terror as my brother was yanked out of the water and spanks landed on his bare bottom. "You're the older brother supposed to be watching over Marc," Dad yelled.

I was too horrified to explain. "But it was me. I was only trying to make the home pretty for mom and baby James, " Dana cried in pain. I wailed for what was happening. My part in bringing beauty home had gone wrong.

I got so wrapped up in what happened. All I could do was crinkle the caramel wrapper as that scene rewound itself repeatedly. "But it was me, I was only trying..." I was a-gawk at how outlandish it was for my brother to get punished for something I did. I almost forgot all about the caramel sitting in the corner of my open mouth. Its sweetness melted into me, and its saltiness pulled me out of my stupor. My memory skipped on, fast-forwarded a notch or two, like a spliced movie film jumping into a whole new scene. Spring moved into fall, and nothing was held in memory until James's baptism.

My memory pulls me into Shortlands Congregational Church. It's set in even richer colors than the night of James's birth. The fire-red bricks of the outside walls bake in deep hues inside. Earthy colors with splashes of royal purple form the nave, and glitters of silver and gold dance around the altar area. All the colors from the flower vases fuse into a glow that shines onto the scene. Mom and Dad are called forward to the baptismal font, baby James in arms, Dana and I clinging to their side. The warmth of family presence fills three pews with aunts and uncles, grandparents and grandma, and so many cousins. I hear Grandpa Stewart unwrapping a hard candy to give to Grandma Stewart.

I am not sure if Dad's hand is guiding the way, or just following the motion, as Mom offers baby James into Reverend Cyril Peat's arms. Dad unruffles the baptismal gown as the minister takes me. Yes, It is as if I am the one being held.

"James, I baptize you in the name of the Father, and of the Son, and of the Holy Ghost."

It is as if I am the one being anointed with water, as if I were being delivered up as a beloved of child. It's the sweetest of memories.

Reverend Peat says, 'This is a moment claimed by God that will be remembered as blessed."

And those who were present that day, any of us, whether 3 years old like me or 73 years old like Great Uncle Joe, perhaps remember that moment of being named and claimed as if they were the one being baptized.

My three-inch Super 8 film reel's worth of earliest memories ends. It's been all too short. I ignore the *flap-flap-flap* of a spinning take-up reel and a bright white screen. Though the caramel has long melted away, a sweetness persists. I am still holding hands with Nana as she assures all will be well as she ushers us to bed. I am still picking flowers in

my eagerness to celebrate life. I am still amazed at
my older brother taking the blame. I am still nestled in the baptism gathering. I am holding my
older brother Dana's hand, and he is holding Dad's
hand, as James is offered back into Mom's arms.
And somehow, I am still blessed!

The last time I preached the "Baptism of Jesus"
Sunday, just a few months ago, I replayed my baptismal memory as I have on so many previous Baptismal Sundays. While preparing the message, I
chewed on a bag of caramels. This candy bag was
a Christmas gift from my baby granddaughter, Ramona. Their sweetness mixed with the saltiness of
my own tears. I wanted to admit that this might
be my last Baptism of Jesus Sunday sermon before
fully retiring, but the words stuck in my throat. I
fervently hoped that I might excite some baptismal
reverie where parishioners felt themselves touched
by blessing. I wanted to bring home the beauty of
the universe. I longed for the sweetness to continue
and imagined holding and splashing baptismal water up to Ramona.

A March 2025 infant amnesia research report
from Yale's Wu Tsai Institute, led by Dr. Nick

Turk-Browne, suggests that retrieving memories from infancy is an "access issue" rather than an "encoding problem" of an underdeveloped brain. I have always said that I don't remember my baptism. Perhaps it is stored so deep away, like an old Super 8 reel falling off a shelf and slipping between the floorboards in my cluttered attic. It seems it could be lost forever. The thought furrows my brow and leaves my mouth dry. Perish that thought. The infant amnesia study explored how babies could show signs of recognition when seeing pictures of scenes that happened with them during the first 2 years of their lives. It makes sense that I remember James's baptism as if it were my own. Perhaps, I was even remembering my own.

I know James's baptism graces so much that is held deep within my heart. Its blessings sweeten the revelries of my memory. It salts my seasons ahead with flavored longings with an assurance that all will be well. That baptism imbued me with a goodness that shows the best in everything else, and it wasn't even mine! I believe there's something there that's enough. It could well be that some deep memory within me has been stirred. It could be that there is something even deeper than memory.

Nothing about baptism has ever been as significant for me as James's baptism at Shortlands Congregational Church, not even when my father officiated the baptisms of each of my three boys in their infancy, and perhaps neither if I were to ever officiate Ramona's baptism. It even overwhelms the fine theological seminary training I received, which touched on the significance of personal baptism as an identity-forming sacrament for Christians. The touch of water on baby James was enough for me. It reminded me of something I knew to be true for my life. It connected me in ways that the air we breathe, the water we drink, and the DNA we share connect with all of life. Perhaps a baptismal touch of water has always been enough, ever since the air quivered above the River Jordan with a voice from the skies saying to those gathered with Jesus, "This is my beloved." How sweet is that!

Six

Manure

By Anne King-Grosh

It is the early spring of the year. I am walking through the pasture on the farm where I grew up, now my brother's farm. I am looking for dried manure patties to take home to add to my compost pile. Already I am dreaming of the beautiful colors of the flowers and the sweetness of the tomatoes that I hope to see growing in my small garden here in Lancaster. I get down to rake up the manure patty, crumbled and dried by winter, entangled with partially digested grass. The physical act of squatting takes me back onto our red dirt street in Addis Ababa, Ethiopia.

I think about the paradoxes that were in the last of many neighborhoods that we lived in during our 14 years there. Beggars and BMWs. Chauffeured diplomats in Mercedes with little flags flying at the windows signifying their importance and women, girls, and boys queuing with plastic buckets waiting their turn for water.

Our home is a dust collector thanks to the dirt street we live on and the trucks that rumble past us to the warehouse a few hundred yards beyond our house. I walk down our short street that ends in a pasture on the outskirts of Addis. I pass a few other houses like ours; small one-story mud and straw-wattled tin-roofed homes, very comfortable and adequate. Closer to the end of the street is an embassy, located in a rented upscale house. It's not as fancy as many embassies in the city, but in contrast to the rest of the homes, it is quite fancy. Very close to the embassy compound is the woman who sells natural fuel–dried manure patties.

I often watch her working in the dry season as I walk. Taking the manure she has collected from the street and pasture nearby, she wets it with water until it is a thick paste. Then with her hands, squatting, she shapes it into a 10-12 inch circle that she places on the ground. Patty after patty, line after line, she works until her small space looks like a filled-in piece of square graph paper. There the patties lie until she turns them over the next day, and then the next day again, until they have been dried by the sun.

When they are dried, she stacks them into piles several feet high. This is her open-air shop for selling cooking fuel.

"May I take your picture? "I asked her one day. "No", she said. "You will just take it and show it to people". I knew what she left unsaid. She knew that her livelihood based on manure patty fuel making would classify her as the "poorest of the poor" and less than second class.

Looking at her diligently dirtying her hands with smelly natural fertilizer, I realize that I have no idea whom she supports by this work. I wonder what her story is? Has she come to the city in hopes of making it rich? Was she born here into a family who relocated from somewhere in the rural area during a famine? Was she deported here from Eritrea during the border war with Ethiopia when both countries did deportations? Is she one of the women who came here as a young girl to work in someone's home and ended up pregnant and thrown out of work?

I will never know. She is not really interested in telling this very personal story to a foreigner whom she is afraid will make her an object in a story and photo for people in a far off country.

Seven

They Call Him Erv...I
Call Him Dad

By Eldon Fry

Angus Wellington Fry left Montana to make a living in the mountains of Idaho. He was a part of the westward movement when homestead property was still available. He met and married the beautiful and Christian woman Bertha Thorton from Leland, Idaho. They were in love, but mixed together like oil and water. Bertha loved church, and Angus never stepped inside a church as far as I knew. He worshipped, or at least was aware of, God in nature. Instead of living in the mountains, they homesteaded in the depths of Bedrock Canyon just below Leland. At the top of the canyon, Idahoans would back up their vehicles or wagons and dump trash. It was a junkyard to neighbors, but at least out of sight for the Frys.

While Bertha was a fine Christian girl, the Thornton family had a reputation for hard drinking, wild living, and using guns to scare city folks. Rumor had it that a local sheriff in Moscow, Idaho, hid under the train depot platform after the Thornton ruffians "shot up" his town.

The Fry homestead was a "hardtack" subsistence in a bedrock location. Bedrock Canyon was stony soil filled with dens of rattlesnakes and other wild animals, and dangerous adventures. Bertha was a strong young woman and battled against the odds, but the lifestyle took its toll. They were in love even though she was seventeen and he was forty. The passionate love of Angus and Bertha gave birth to Inettta, a beautiful red-haired daughter whose slight build did not give a hint of her toughness. Five years later, Ervin, a red-haired delight to his parents, was born. Bedrock Canyon living was a hard life for the parents, who began to drink too much. Arguments turned into dish-throwing fights, yelling expletives, and screaming threats that were no longer loving. The old clapboard house was not a safe place for kids or really for the adults.

Two animals provided safe space for young Ervin in those early years: his dog, Prince, and his pinto horse, Ribbon. He was free to saddle up his horse when work was accomplished, and he could ride for hours in the silence of his thoughts and awareness of surrounding nature. His horse was the envy of some friends and a source of pride for the "kid". His dog was an attentive listener when Ervin whispered his frustrations and stories about his interest in girls or imagined stories of what the future might hold. Prince was faithful and trained by Ervin to help gather up cows, hunt rabbits, and identify the danger of snakes or predators. Prince became his only confidant in the isolation of the canyon.

His father used horses and mules for field work and transportation during the preschool years. Ervin was expected to help on the farm as a child-adult. He knew how to handle a team of horses and learned the rough language needed to control mules. It was hard work that built strong muscles and raging confidence. During times of recreation, Ervin gathered wild berries or fresh fruit from the trees on the canyon hillsides. That became a respite for Ervin into adulthood when he would show up with a hatful of berries or saddlebags full of apples after "checking" on his cows. Ervin viewed it as his private Garden of Eden. He learned how to escape the deadly danger of snakes. As a child, he often suffered correction from a branch cut from a nearby shrub or tree that his mother wielded in anger. His father preferred to use his leather belt. Any lack of obedience to rules resulted in corporal punishment to correct his misguided ways. For Ervin, this was an accepted and expected way of life.

Although intimacy was not available with his mother and father in their busyness of survival and desperation of poverty, Ervin sensed love from his father and mother through their diligent work. Hard work became his love language. At one point, he recalled that his father walked out of the canyon for ten miles to labor for someone at the rate of one dollar for a day's work. His mother would occasionally but rarely share from her sparse purse some coins for a treat at the grocery store fifteen miles away. Angus was not a good farmer, but he was a superb outdoorsman. Angus would unhook the farm equipment, park the horses or mules in the barn, and leave the farmstead for ten days to two weeks to hunt for game to feed the family. Ervin managed the farm in his father's absence. Anger seethed below the surface of his parents and would pour out without restraint. Expletives we yelled toward each other on occasions of binge drinking or wild parties. Many arguments were triggered by accusations of who danced closest to whom at the dance. His sister, Inetta, was bossy and controlling of her younger sibling. She became a "yeller" modeled after her parents. Ervin's dog died trying to protect him from a rattlesnake. But unfortunately, his dog could not protect him from the sexual abuse of a visiting relative who threatened his life if he ever told anyone. That secret remained locked in Ervin's memory for almost eight decades and churned below the surface of his life decisions. A friend of his Christian mother invited Ervin to her Sunday School Class at Leland Pioneer Community Church. It was a small congregation at the mouth of Bedrock Canyon. But it proved to be a friendly respite when he could attend. Ervin enjoyed the lessons and the friendship of his mother's friend. He rode his horse up the steep climb out of the canyon alone on those Sundays he could go to church. His sister never joined him at church or on his trips to school. She was needed for survival at home. She was withdrawn and angry at God and her context. Later, Ervin would wonder if she had been emotionally, physically, or even sexually abused during those times he was not at home. It remained an unspoken pain between these two siblings over their lifetime.

School was a relief from the rigors of life in Bedrock. Ervin rode his horse out of the canyon to Southwick school with tie racks and sheds for horses that students rode to class. At that time, before the schoolhouse burned down, it had elementary and high school facilities. It included a cafeteria that served home-baked meals and even a small gymnasium that served as a community gath-

ering place for special events. Ervin was a mischie-
vous student who never really learned to read well
but was excellent with ciphers. Ervin seemed to
make friends easily and embraced some of the curi-
ous exploits of young children. He and his friends
would tip over the outdoor toilets by tying ropes to
their saddles and stretching the rope between their
horses on Halloween night. They played school-
yard games, teased girls, and bragged about accom-
plishments. It was there that friends began to
shorten his name to "Erv". He was their pal. Erv's
stubbornness led to clashes with the school principal. Somehow, he gained the appreciation of teach-
ers and other students. But school days would
soon be past because of a nightmarish event on the
horizon.

One afternoon, his father, in a fit of rage, ac-
cused Ervin of not doing a chore before dinner.
Ervin responded in anger like a cornered wild an-
imal. "I am NOT guilty!" he insisted. That de-
fensiveness became gas poured on a blazing fire.
His father beat Ervin with the buckle end of the
dreaded belt until Ervin could not stand. Then his
father left for the fields and Ervin left home for-

ever. He rode Ribbon about fifteen miles to his grandparents and stumbled into their house. He recovered in bed for two weeks until the wounds had started to heal. Then Ervin slowly recuperated over several weeks until his grandparents felt he was well enough to return to school. But the principal who had clashed with Ervin previously would not allow him to return mid-semester. Ervin lived with his grandparents for the end of the semester. In a fit of rage, Ervin turned to the principal, who relented and offered Ervin a path to return. Ervin seethed with anger and refused the offer. He never completed any more schooling beyond the sixth grade. He was an angry young man deeply wounded by the system. He felt he was being treated unfairly and took it personally.

A good Lutheran family named Finke, that operated a successful logging business, took him into their home with a foster-like parent agreement. It was not an adoption or permanent, but rather through high school age. He never belonged and always felt the difference in the family dynamics. The Finkes were kind to him and appreciated his work ethic. But he knew their two sons were a

priority and would inherit the logging business.
He grew up sensing that lack of full acceptance.
Ervin embraced the idea that he would always be
an outsider. He felt the need to work with perfection to be appreciated. Ervin did work for the
Finkes throughout his lifetime, between other
jobs. The need for perfection to be accepted carried
over into his adult years. He pushed my brother
and me to follow that pattern. Once my brother
and I returned to Idaho, we helped him get ready
for the winter season. His fences were in bad
shape, with the barbed wire drooping, and the
cows would escape, trying to feed on the neighbor's grass. We fixed the fence so the cattle would
not get out, and when Dad went to town, we decided we would also replace the rickety barbed wire
gates. When he returned, his only comment was
"the posts are too big for a gate." My brother
looked at me and said, "Nothing has changed."
Perfectionism infected his life and, at times, raised
the hackles of his sons. Even Ervin's faith lent itself
to holiness, a form of Christian perfectionism that
grew into legalism and an understanding of God as

just waiting for a human mistake to be made, and punishment was certain.

When Ervin left the Finkes, he traveled to Oregon to log with his uncle, who was about the same age. Both had red hair and personalities that matched the stereotype of a hotheaded redhead. They were "hellraisers" and met and socialized with some famous gangsters at the places they frequented on weekends. The stories of those years were wild but seldom recounted because of the embarrassment of the lifestyle. That was especially true after both men became men of faith.

Ervin eventually left Oregon and returned to Southwick and fell in love with Alice Benjamin, who was rebelling against the religion of her family and its form of Christian legalism. Ervin had a "bad boy" image that attracted Alice, and they were married in 1945 in a simple ceremony in the Benjamin home. The first two years, Alilce and I lived with my grandparents while Ervin worked on a big ranch in Oregon. Ervin saved enough money to buy a "fixer-upper" house in Southwick that had no running water and only four cornerstones to hold the box house up instead of a foundation.

I was born a little over a year later in Lewiston's St. Joseph's Hospital. My mother nearly died in the process and was in the hospital for weeks. The doctor said, "You can never have another child." This set the stage for my parents to adopt a little brother from the Lewiston Children's Home. Both parents had come to faith at Haven of Rest Crusade and walked the sawdust aisle and prayed with a counselor. That changed the dynamics of our family. Dad no longer went fishing on Sunday and we were at church every time the doors were open at Southwick Community Church. My parents were attracted to the holiness movement with camps and crusades and its call to a legalistic perfection which I could not tolerate.

My father provided a very basic three-room house for his maternal grandmother Thorton. He cared for her until she died, even when no one else in the family would do so. I would chop wood and visit her daily, making sure that all was well. The church was the center of their lives until they proved that the parsonage sewer leaked into our drinking water from the well that my dad had drilled through solid rock. That realization created angry and tense arguments. Finally, my parents joined the Pilgrim Holiness Church in Clarkston, Washington, which was sixty miles away. I recall the days of battling over water and leaving neighborhood friends for church down in the city. That was one of many battles my father experienced, which only served to marginalize him more. Those arguments prevented him from fully engaging with issues. It was simpler for him to just work harder. He worked at a "planer mill" for several years, had a small herd of cattle (12 or so) and a couple of horses, and always a mule, and even rented some land to farm with ancient machinery. I laughingly said he knew every cow's birthday but none of his boys' or wife's birth dates. I was a captain of the football team and a four-year letterman in basketball, plus baseball and even track, yet he never saw one game nor cared to talk about them. He viewed my Saturday events as an interruption in his lifestyle.

Our place of connection was hunting together and building a fence for the cattle pasture. He had closed off emotionally enough through the years that he did not know how to communicate with his young sons. He tried to communicate love by working hard, always keeping busy, and expecting his boys to do the same. Alice's mom was a valedictorian of her class, a motivated teacher in the church, and even represented the church at denominational levels. The clash of backgrounds created sparks of misunderstanding between them, which they seemed capable of talking out. But for my brother and me, my father had no ability to help us understand or connect with the impact of his background, or for him to be present in our dilemmas. My mother knew how to speak love, but my father did not have that capacity.

I recall my father being hit by a windfall tree while logging. The tree smashed his arm, hurt his back, his head, and caused multiple other wounds. Doctors did not think he would survive. Because of the time it took to get him off the mountain and carried over logging roads to the nearest hospital, survival was questionable. Doctors said it was a miracle he survived. He returned home after a long hospital stay, where they patched up broken bones that they had left untreated because they did not think he would live. His right arm could not rotate properly. The arm had an obvious bone graft. Then came the devastating blow and discovery that the insurance was fraudulent, so our family faced big medical bills, and deep in Ervin's soul, it confirmed that he could not trust "the man." He became suspicious of big business and offers. He was restless when he returned home. His identity as a "busy man" who worked hard for his family was lost. He struggled with worth and who he was as a husband and father. We learned to live on the tiny workman's comp monies. Ervin decided he would help a neighbor in desperate need of someone to help. He was careful not to violate any rules beyond the limits of workman's comp. An anonymous neighbor from the small community reported him as working so even the small stipend we were surviving on was taken away. It added to the disappointment and distrust he had experienced earlier when he attempted to arrange with the Kendrick bank to purchase a plot of land. But they determined he was too young and did not have enough collateral. In the meantime, he was undermined by relatives who were the richest family in town. Trust did not come easily for Ervin after those incidents.

I misunderstood his hesitancy at times. The children of some of those people were my friends in school. I was confused by his actions. My father was firm in his faith to help and love others, but sometimes that love was confrontational. I could not understand or comprehend the complexity of all of that. My parents welcomed crusty ranchers and loggers into our house. I recall my dad arguing with one such friend about a fence that had allowed cattle from free range to intermingle with those being held for special breeding. It was an angry and threatening confrontation. It seemed to be on the verge of fists or guns, yet that very same person came to our house and ate with us and told wonderful stories that created peals of laughter. My father would help him move his cattle, fix his fence, and call him a friend.

The life experiences left my father with complex feelings at one level, informed by faith and love, that refused to conform to the world and context of our mountain "unincorporated" village. His lifestyle impressed some others in our town of fifty. In later years, Dad received a plaque as a gift from a neighbor that announced, "**Mayor of Southwick**." Dad had it hung outside by our porch door. Dad respected our Native American neighbors. Many times I saw him slip money to an American Indian family in desperate need even when we had little. People were welcomed to come by to fill up water tanks, drink coffee, and maybe eat lunch or fresh baked goods without paying anything. While I enjoyed interacting with various visitors, I was fortunate to see my parents working together in hospitality and not at odds with each other.

My father was a lifelong Democrat. George Brocke was a local state Democratic representative. He was a significant businessman in the town just ten miles down the mountain. However, a Democratic program for farmers was giving grants for storm damage to local crops. My father walked into the Democratic run government office in Lewiston to claim his benefit, but the person behind the desk laughed at him and said his "farm was too small to consider." Dad left the office as a Republican the rest of his life. As I reflect on that sudden change, I realize that my father was always an advocate for the marginalized and the "little" guy. He could not cope with his disappointment that the Democrat program was not for the "little guy."

Because of the seasonal nature of logging, my father took a job at the local planer mill in Ahsahka. That is where rough boards are smoothed and sized and sent to areas needing lumber for construction. Dad had many stories from those days and would laugh as he told them until tears rolled down his face. He told of a co-worker named Fritz who lived in the woods. A bear whose head was stuck in a bucket was frantically banging into objects on the ranch. The racket awakened Fritz. He found his stored ancient rifle and shot the bear. Fritz was so impressed with himself that he had his gun made into a masterpiece to put over the mantel of his fireplace. He told another story of Fritz, who saw a car parked out in front of his rural house on a summer night. Fritz stuck his head in the open window and asked, "Need any help?" The response was a fist in his eye from the couple "making out" in the front seat. Fritz commented later, "I guess they needed no help." Dad would tell stories of "his big Swede," a working partner at the mill. Dad at 5'9" was matched with a muscular Swedish man over six foot tall. He still had a Swedish brogue. Dad would try to duplicate the conversations like "I tell you Oiven, ve pack this car and rest together." Dad's favorite story was from his logging days, where the crew ate together because they were away from home for a week at a time. One Swedish immigrant said, "Pass the yelly." When informed, it was Jam. He said, "By golly, I just learned to say 'yelly' and now you call it 'yam". Even in the darkest of times, Dad could tell a good story and laugh until tears ran down his cheeks. I think it was natural for him, but it was also a medication for the pain below the surface. Even as a teenager in the home, I did not really understand the history of pain and rough experiences of my father as he grew up.. Dad did not understand this kid who was always reading instead of doing something. When I tried to complete chores in a timely manner, it was to avoid the criticism and even anger of my father. I never developed a deep love for horses, cows, or certainly mules like my dad. But I learned to be a trusted caretaker much as he had in his father's absences.

Dad was vocal in his anger toward big farmers and land purchased for corporate "tax write-offs." He argued against the overuse of fertilizer that replaced natural fertilizer and allowed for the non-rotation of farms and weed spraying by planes that not only sickened animals and natural greenery but also sickened people as well. He argued that plants in fence rows were needed to maintain wildlife and provide food for pheasants, deer, and other wildlife. At the same time, he did not trust institutions to treat people fairly so he was never a part of an organization or system that could fight for justice. On a personal basis, he was kind to native Americans, shopped at locally owned stores rather than using chain stores in bigger towns. In later years, he ate breakfast regularly at a Native American-owned restaurant as one way to support people on the local Nez Perce reservation. He took in a nephew who was estranged from his father and cared for him through the wild years of high school. When Dad died, Doug was the only relative who helped me care for the things left behind. He even adopted Dad's precious mule and cared for it until the mule died. Dad was a hoarder of sorts because you might need whatever he collected for reuse later. I did not fully comprehend the poverty and lifestyle that my dad had experienced in the desperation to eke out a living in the canyon homestead. Doug helped me sort through the piles of "saved" items to determine what might need to be kept. Doug helped lift and to store heavy items and knew some of the people I would need to contact who would be interested in the piles of "junk."

Vietnam created a dilemma for Dad. My brother Warren served two tours and received several medals, including the Bronze Star. When he returned to California, he was spit on and called unrepeatable names. He returned with undiagnosed PTSD. My brother married someone with children who was an active part of the California drug culture. They moved to the mountains of Idaho, close to my parents, but were unprepared for the challenges. Vietnam had taught my brother that any day he could die. When my brother received a paycheck, he spent it all. Then, the bill

collectors called my parents searching for Warren.
His wife returned to the allure of drugs in California. In anger, my father disassociated from my
brother even though my brother had divorced and
remarried and lived in Anacortes, WA., hundreds
of miles from Idaho. One Fall, my wife and I came
to help my parents prepare for the winter season.
We determined that we would travel on to Anacortes to spend time with Warren and his bride,
Dyna. Dad and Mom were faced with a challenge
and prayed together. They finally decided they
would join us to see Warren, Dyna, and family,
now eight in number (his, hers, and theirs). Rec-
onciliation took place over those several days and
healed our family. When Warren was killed later in
an explosion at work several years later, we grieved
together as a family. The process of grief revealed
the importance of healing that had occurred earlier.

Dad had a brother, Ted, born 20 years after
my dad. They did not grow up together, but Dad
loved Ted, who was closer to my age than his. Over
the years, Dad kept in touch with Ted and his family. Ted was in the Air Force and planned to return

to Japan as a missionary after retiring. Ted died of a heart condition and left a widow and two small children. It was a meaningful day when Dad was privileged to walk Laura, his niece, down the aisle for her wedding. It filled a void of only sons for Dad.

I was caught in the polarities of caring for justice issues of the marginalized and oppressed, yet my dad did not trust institutions to be helpful in support of those people who needed it most. Dad also had a compassionate heart for displaced or abused/wounded animals. He rescued two dogs left as helpless puppies on a local farm. He trained them and cared for them until he had to finally leave his home for the hospital then care center. He was always compassionate for the "underdogs" in life at a personal level.

Dad's "conversion" experience truly led him to forgive his father and others for offenses through the years. I am grateful for this part of his story. I saw the transformative power of grace. Even to those who had undermined and rejected him earlier in life. Bitterness was absent from his life. He carried regrets but not unforgiveness. Dad was careful about trust and levels of friendship with those who mistreated him but forgiving. His life was filled with integrity. The Southwick general store owner, Clay King, told him that many people had asked for credit during lean years and now they had money but never paid off those bills. He went on to say, "Erv, I knew there were times you were desperate and had to ask for credit but you were always someone who paid off your bills." That is an important part of my heritage and challenges me to be a person who keeps my word as much as possible.

Yet like all relationships, there were misunderstandings and tension at times. I recall helping my father with a Jeep he had been restoring. As we pushed it from the garage, it bumped something harmlessly, and Dad reverted to perfection mode. His comment was sharp and hurtful. I turned and said, "Dad, I am not your enemy!" He quickly returned to a friendly pose and apologized. Another turning point came as I visited him for the final time in the care center. A great aunt called him. I could tell she asked about me and said, "You should be really proud of him." My dad answered,

"Yes, I am really proud of him." That was something that released pent-up emotions for me, as I had never felt good enough or been told he understood any of the honors I achieved.

He grew up without intimacy and never said, "I love you". He felt working hard, said "I love you." When I moved to Pennsylvania to work at Messiah University, I ended a phone call with him by saying, "I love you." After a long pause, he said, "Me too," and hung up. But in the ensuing years, he concluded our conversations by saying, "I love you," and he would even hug me when I visited him, usually shedding tears. So much healing on my end took place in those moments as I began to understand how he had bravely crossed emotional and social barriers to share his love in that way. As I have reflected on Erv, my dad, I realize that he faced a new world and adapted to its challenges with bravery and determination. I now can admire his courage and appreciate his imperfections to resist the messages of his childhood, to relate to me, even though he might not understand me.

In the final days of his life, he was in a private room in a care center and experienced "mini strokes". He talked to me and his nurses about being visited by this white horse yet it would run off before he could ride it. It was a space between a dream and reality for him. When his nurse called me to inform of his death at the hospital after another mini-stroke, she simply said, "I think this time when the white horse came for Ervin, he got on him and simply rode away." That image remains today. His friends and community called him Erv, shortened for respect, but I lovingly and gratefully call him dad.

The Story I Tell

As I sit here at my desk, remembering my dad, I have many stories I could tell. I hear his voice when I make decisions. There have been times I have asked myself, "What would Dad do here?" The answer is often apparent. I vividly recall his infectious laughter after telling a good story, and it still brings smiles and encourages me to tell stories. I appreciate how he broke off the chains of abuse and marginalization. That gives me confidence to move ahead in life even when I know my limitations, faults, and failures. When I return to Idaho and go by Bedrock Canyon, I find it easier to pray in "Big

Sky country" than anywhere else in the world. My last visit there, the old clapboard house was still standing in the midst of green fruit trees and beautiful wildflowers that hid the rocky soil and rattlesnake dangers in the canyon floor. I also hear the echoes of Dad's voice down the hallways of time and realize that he was dropped into a canyon society in "red neck" culture. He rode out of that canyon to a different world that he adjusted to for survival. Dad thrived imperfectly as he adapted. I realize that at times I did not know my dad, and he could not understand me or relate to my world.

At night, I turn on a CD that has different groups singing older hymns. In my heart and memory, I can hear my father joining my multi-talented mother to sing at family gatherings and Christian meetings. Because of their lifestyle choices, the songs have become meaningful and authentic over my years. That is the story I tell. Here are some life lesson observations

1. Abuse does not need to be generational. *(My father broke this cycle)*

2. While a father's absence impacts a child, it does not determine their future. (My father's absence did not keep me from learning from others.)

3. Joy can sustain people through traumatic events, *giving them hope. (Joy contributed to healing in my dad's life and has been for me as well.)*

4. Love languages are often developed with the context of our lives. *(The development of work as a love language impacted my father and he passed it on. It has not been an easy shift for me from "workaholism.")*

5. Our life experiences influence our theology. *(Perfectionism developed from a sociological context became a spiritual motivation for dad.)*

6. Love can change the course of a child's life. *(I am grateful that the Finkes expanded the boundary of family to impact my father.)*

7. We need community to make a difference and to deal with injustice. *(My dad battled injustice but lacked the connections to make systemic change.)*

8. All human life should be respected. *(My father modeled respect for other marginalized people and my life was enriched by diversity.)*

9. God is capable of transforming lives. *(The radical difference between early dad and later dad is an affirmation of the power of God to transform us.)*

10. Forgiveness does indeed cover a multitude of sins. *(As my father forgave his father and mother and family, my life was impacted by health and opportunity. I have been challenged to forgive rather than cling to the pain of past hurts.)*

Eight

The Baton

By Cheryl Stewart

I am not sure why I was so adamant about trying out. I had not had the opportunity to. . . there had not been money to. . . take lessons in dance or gymnastics or baton twirling. I knew no one who could teach me. . . but I had heard the announcement that there were going to be tryouts for majorettes, and I wanted to try out. I wanted to be one of those pretty girls in sparkling swimsuits who led the band.

I started practicing right away on my toy baton. Then, in a few days, my mother brought me home a new, sparkly, balanced baton. I knew that there usually wasn't money in our family for extras like batons. My parents had gone without something to buy this. . .

After spending hours practicing after school and on weekends for a month, I was dropping the baton less, and I had figured out two twirls: a two-handed twirl and an over and under one-handed twirl. . . and with these, I made up a "routine."

On the day of tryouts, I woke up excited. As I left the house to walk to school, my father said, "I hope the tryouts go well."

It took a lot of patience that day to sit through classes; the tryouts would be after school. Finally, I entered the familiar, enormous, reverberating gym.

There were seven of us girls who had shown up, and Mrs. Barnes told us that there would be six of us who would make the team.

Mrs. Barnes called me up to be the first one to try out. I was proud and hopeful as I stepped out with my sparkly baton. I did my over and under one-handed twirl and my two-handed twirl in various combinations. I walked forward and backward. Around and around that large, brown gym I walked. I looked at my baton in concentration as I twirled and walked.

And then, it was over. I hadn't really been that scared. I had done my routine as practiced. I hadn't dropped my baton, not even once. I felt pretty good. The audience politely clapped.

The next girl to try out was Shelby. She had been on the team the year before. Shelby didn't look at her baton; she looked at us, the audience. . . and Shelby smiled. And Shelby didn't walk around and around the gym; she marched. "March," I thought. "Why didn't I think of that?"

Shelby did the two twirls I had done, and four or five more. Shelby could throw her baton up into the air, spin around, catch it, keep on twirling, and not miss a beat. When Shelby finished, everyone clapped enthusiastically.

And then, the next girl got up, the new girl, Josie. She had obviously had baton twirling experience at her previous school.

And so it went. What had been an exciting dream was turning into a nightmare. If I held any scrap of hope that any of the remaining girls would be worse than I, and that I would still make the team, that hope was dispelled in the next interminable 45 minutes. Each girl marched, smiled, and twirled. Each girl threw her baton up into the air and caught it at least once.

I didn't want to be there anymore in that gym. I wished I could disappear into thin air. . . Poof!

I wanted to be anywhere else. Yet, I was a girl who followed the rules, and to get up and leave would be unexpected and impolite.

And so I stayed and endured the horrible ordeal. . until all of the girls had tried out, until the three judges had conferred. . . until Mrs. Barnes read out the names of the six girls who had made the team. . . until there was the recognition that my name, of course, had not been included.

Only then did I get up and walk back home so sad, deflated, and embarrassed.

When I arrived home, my father asked me how it went. "I didn't make the team," I said. I was afraid you might not make the team," he said.

And then, I went to my room. Part of me wanted to scream or cry or beat the wall, but I hadn't been brought up to do these. Not a tear escaped. I just lay on my bed for a long while.

"Why, if my father thought I might not make the team," I wondered, "Why then hadn't he stopped me? Why had he let me go?" But, oh, no. I realized that both he and I knew that no one could have stopped me, considering how determined I had been.

And I knew deep down that I would never twirl or even touch that sparkly, balanced baton again!

Nine

Jefari's Grandaughter

By Anne King-Grosh

I look at Kate, our 18-year-old beautiful daughter. How did she get to be this old and grown up? Whatever happened to all those years? I look more closely at her and see her facial features. The beautiful, slightly long and narrow face has a nose she thinks is too big, but which looks just right to me. What genes gave her her face, her petite stature, and her wonderful writing skills? Whose DNA influenced the strength of her voice?

I remember the day she said, "Mom, do you think my birth mother was like Jafari 'cause I really hope not".

Jefari was our next-door neighbor. To get to her mud-walled, tin-roofed house, one needed to go out of our compound gate, abruptly turn left, and then go through the open fence into her compound. A well-worn dirt path took me to her house. In the dry season, it was a great path, but in the rainy season, it was better to take big steps from one tuft of grass to another.

Jefari always had numerous children around the house. Some of them were hers, some were her daughters'. They missed school for many reasons, sometimes because they had no money for school uniforms or exercise books. Money was scarce. Jefari's husband was many years older than she was and was too sick to work. A few older children got daily laborer-type jobs and helped to support the family. I never figured out how they lived, ate, or even bought coffee beans.

Like many other Ethiopian women, Jefari roasted a handful of coffee beans daily. Often, she had only enough money to buy a handful, so one of the children would be given a coin and sent to a nearby, very small shop. The shop had a window through which the transaction would be made.

Inside the shop were a few shelves with matches, candles, salt, small cans of Blue Band margarine, and a small assortment of spices for making the traditional wat. Sugar could also be purchased in plastic bags, or for a few cents, one could buy a few tablespoons poured into a rolled-up paper that looked much like a miniature ice cream cone.

Many days, the smell of roasting coffee wafted through the air over the stone block wall that separated our compound from Jefari's, and I would think, *I know just how it looks in their home right now. Jefari is sitting at a small charcoal burner. She is sitting on a backless stool, bending over, moving the green beans back and forth on a little round flat metal dish. As the beans get hot, they turn dark brown and oily. The smoke coming from the beans smells like fresh coffee. She stops and pushes a bean that isn't darkening like the rest into her hand. She throws that one away and keeps moving the beans so they don't get burned. Now they are finished. I can hear someone pounding the beans, crushing them in the mortar and pestle until they are ground into a fine powder. Now someone has gone out to the faucet in the yard and is getting water to pour into the jebana. But before the water is poured in, the coffee powder is carefully scooped out of the pestle and, with a cupped hand, tapped into the mouth of the jebana. Now the jebana goes onto the charcoal fire, and the sinnis, the small demitasse cups, are gathered onto the small buna serving board.* Ah, the smell of fresh roasted coffee, the pounding sound, the gathering of the family to sit and drink together...there is no rush, no hurry.

But today I don't drink coffee with Jafari and her family. Today I am in her home because her grandchild is dying. I heard the news from one of the daughters, so I went over to the house to sit with Jefari for a while. When I enter the first room, for the home has only 3 rooms with a very uneven dirt floor, I see Jefari sitting on a chair holding her granddaughter. I didn't even know this child was sick, but it's clear that she is not only sick but is dying. Jefari is sitting very still, saying nothing, just patiently waiting there. Her only movement is from her right hand, with which she strokes the little girl's eyelids shut each time they open. Her eyelids fall open, Jefari strokes them shut. They fall open again. Jefari strokes them shut. Open and shut, open and shut. It's a rhythm with no sound, except for the irregular breathing of the little girl. Nor is there any movement other than that of Jefaris' hand stroking the little girl's eyes shut. I sit there thinking, *I am a nurse in the US. I would be throwing this girl into the car and rushing her to the ER. Or, I would call 911 and frantically count the minutes until someone arrives to take over with life support. But here, it is already too late for medical help to make a difference. This is what I can do: sit here quietly and at peace. Sit with Jefari as her neighbor.*

Jefari's steady stroking of her granddaughter's eyes mesmerizes me. There is a peace about it, a peace with the finality of this death.

Finally, 30 minutes later, the quiet is broken. Jefari says, "You may go now". I have been asked to leave, so I do. I am gone for only a short time until the wailing begins. The granddaughter has died.

Ten

The Turtle

By Jack Scandrett

"Phew! That was close! Scary, stupid close! I was so careless," the turtle said to himself, struggling to catch his breath. The deeper he dove, the more relieved he felt. He was grateful to be alive. His thankfulness was beyond what words could describe. Just then, however, a memory flashed in his mind. He remembered the tragic, horrible death of his younger brother. He could yet see the desperate, frightened, help me look on his brother's face as he was hauled onto the shore. Though it was several years ago, it seems like it was yesterday. The boys beat him with clubs until his lovely amber eyes went black. Lifeless! His body broken, shell shattered, and the blood. In the recesses of his mind, the laughter of the boys who took his brother's life still haunted him. It was a senseless death. A mockery of life," he believed. His beautiful brother was simply abandoned on the beach for the scavengers to feast upon. A deep sadness filled him. And a reprieve! This could have been his fate as well.

The turtle was bleeding around the mouth where the hook tore loose. "But that will heal in time," he thought. 'I have experienced fish hooks before." One other time, near the Bahamas, he was briefly snagged while swimming in the kelp.

He felt exhausted. Spent. His flippers ached. The monofilament line had cut deep into his right flipper. The man was strong and determined to see the turtle's demise. "I thought for sure I would crash against the rocks. The man with the fishing rod seemed so angry. The boy looked distressed. Then peaceful. The praying man was smiling. Whomever they were is of no mind to me now. I am free!" As he swam away, these were some of the thoughts that quivered through his being.

The turtle was grateful and vowed never to be deceived again, no matter how hungry.

Jack knew that one day, he, too, would be free. With help, his wounds would heal. The inner tranquility of heart, body, and mind would replace the mental anguish he experienced. His spirit would be renewed and refreshed. He knew that one day, he would discover true parental love and the meaning of life. And one day, Jack will also understand Richard's death, visit his resting place, and grieve a beautiful life violently cut short.

Eleven

God Calls Us To Remember

By Ruth Martin

But God doesn't want us to remember in order to condemn us—to lock us in a state of self-hate. God calls us to remember so that we can be drawn in, so that we may be healed and freed, so that we may move forward through the pain and not around it. (Britney Winn Lee)

Seventy-two years have passed, and the image is stationary in my memory.

A woman in a long dark dress that almost touches the floor is standing at the kitchen door. She is wearing a black bonnet and a black shawl. Standing at her side is a young girl also wearing a long dress and dark bonnet. The woman reaches out and takes the baby from a man whose face is hidden. The woman with the baby follows; the young girl follows. The door closes. No words are exchanged. The memory remains a frozen numbness. The haunting silence is deafening.

My response now: I am sure there was a conversation and tears. I am equally convinced my mother was present. The man, I am sure, was my father. I wonder what days were like that followed. Why do I know so few details?

My mother was incapacitated with severe upper-body burns. She sustained the burns while starting a fire in the kitchen stove at 5 AM. She had both hands, forearms, and upper arms bandaged. Within a few weeks, she went through childbirth. My father had the usual farm work and daily family responsibilities, which my mother could not do.

The memory haunts me now, as I never asked my mother or my father:

"How was that for you?" "How did you get through those days?"

How did you get through that challenge?"

Did I ever consider or think of asking? "What were you feeling? Who supported you those days?"

Filled with emotion, another memory. It was June 27, 2005, and I was standing at my mother's graveside listening to the minister's meditation on Psalm 23. I was engaged in an internal conversation with my mother – believed, hoped she heard my lament:

"I am so sorry I did not get to know you, your heart!

I know so little about you.

What did you think about and/or pray about during wakeful nights?

What brought you joy?

What troubled you?

What were your hopes for your family, your children, for me?"

Momentarily, I hear the minister's voice reading Psalm 23: "*Der HERR ist mein Hirte; mir wird nichts mangeln.*

Then, warm tears bubble up, slide down my cheeks. The internal dialogue continued:

"Mom, I am so sorry. So, so sorry."

Softly, quietly, within me, a deep knowing emerges—not an audible sound, not a thought, but certainly an unshakeable knowing.

"She knows it all now! She knows it all, she knows you really care, and you cared deeply that life was often difficult. She knows you did not have the words or the know-how to express your caring. She knows!"

That was a transforming experience—a deeply healing moment. I felt God's love and care deeply and still do. I know my mother knows—she knows my sadness and my caring.

Again, this day, as I contemplate the meaning of this fixed memory of my newborn brother leaving with my Aunt Anna, I take comfort in the fact that she knows I care.

"Mom knows it all now – my misgivings, my thoughtlessness. She knows –

She knows I did care and do care."

This I call to mind, and therefore I have hope:
The steadfast love of the Lord never ceases, his
mercies never come to an end;
they are new every morning; great is your faithful-
ness.
Lamentations 3:21-23 (NRSVUE)

Twelve

A Return To Security

By Charles E. Gardner

A woman holds a babe to her breast, cradling him in both arms, and looking down at him lovingly. He is wrapped in a thick, soft blanket and has a contented expression on his face. The babe is me, not just as an infant, but also as a child, adolescent, and teenager. The woman represents the world as I experienced it from birth through age eighteen. Secure best describes my state of existence throughout those years.

The security came mainly from the family into which I was born. A stay-at-home, emotionally stable mother provided my care in my formative years. A home-evenings-and-weekends father mentored me as I matured. Though imperfect, they interacted with me in ways that let me know I was valued, respected, and loved. The basic needs of food and shelter were never in doubt. There was never a time when I feared either of them would leave the family. Beyond my family, the world also seemed a safe place to exist, despite concerns over "the bomb" that were prevalent in the fifties and sixties.

A shift, at first barely perceptible, occurred around my eighteenth birthday. Two events caused the shift. The first was expected when I left my family in September to live in Ithaca, New York, and begin studies at Cornell. The second, unexpected, occurred on November 25th, when I married my high school sweetheart to form a new family.

Living in a new location, with a new partner, and a child coming soon brought dramatic differences, yet the same sense of security remained. Despite reasonable concerns, my parents committed to supporting us financially so that I could continue pursuing my education. I was now married to the person I loved, and felt the love reciprocated. I was confident that my new family would duplicate my previous one, providing a safe environment for all. Chuck was born in May of 1968.

This state of being continued through the college years. Tanya was born in June of 1971, and all was well. Graduation and my first job came to pass two years later. Then, gradually, cracks appeared in the new family foundation over the next twenty years. George was born in December 1973 but suffered multiple birth defects and lived only a few hours. Lara entered the world in May of 1976, and then Meredith in June of 1981. Our family was now complete, but the security had definitely evaporated.

Chuck began demonstrating anti-social behaviors at home and in school. Alenda and I found ourselves arguing over money, which was always in short supply. The security that I desired for our family steadily slipped away. Moving to a new home provided excitement in 1992, but family conflict continued.

A low point came after Chuck married and became a father in 1995, then was sentenced to five years in prison for assaulting his wife. Alenda and I were emotionally disconnected and, at times, openly hostile to each other. Meredith was in high school and mired in substance abuse. Tanya was now pursuing her career, and Lara was in college, and both suffered anxiety knowing their family of origin was a mess. I recall driving to work many mornings, feeling a hard knot in the center of my abdomen as an indication of my stress. Alenda and I went for counseling, but initially found no relief.

And then, slowly, ever so slowly, things began to improve. At first, it was only between Alenda and me. Neither of us recalls anything from our counseling sessions that triggered the improvement, but our relationship healed. Chuck was released from prison with a greatly reduced level of anger. His wife took him back, and he has lived a positive life ever since. Meredith continued to struggle until she became pregnant, and then the miracle of life within her womb led her to cease self-destructive actions. Tanya and Lara continued to navigate life's challenges successfully.

This improved state continued for several years, until Alenda and I retired in 2015. A significant event occurred in July of that year, when we were at a restaurant making final plans for a "bucket list" vacation. We each got out our phones and entered the departure date. And then I started to cry. And cry some more. And then some more. I could not stop, yet had no idea why I was crying. Alenda was also clueless and sat, looking at me with a caring expression, yet too perplexed to do anything more. I eventually returned to normal, and we finished our meal.

Over the next few days, I understood the source of the tears. My subconscious harbored a notion of what a family should be. It should provide security, including financial security, so that all members can feel emotionally comfortable, expressing themselves in words and actions as God created them to do. When our family proved incapable of doing that, I took it as a personal failure. Sitting in that restaurant, once again secure in my marriage, with adequate financial reserves and good relationships with all my children and grandchildren, I finalized plans for a dream vacation. Relief and tears broke through. I had made it.

Thirteen

Nazareth

By Jewel Showalter

I was sitting at a long table filled with light and dark-skinned people. Colorful dishes filled with spicy red meat, soft yellow lentils, potatoes, cabbage, and carrots lined the center of the table. A gray, spongy crepe-bread lay folded beside my plate. I liked my plate. It was enamel-covered metal with bright blue swirls. But there was nothing to drink.

I was hungry and stuffed the sour crepe and spicy chicken leg into my mouth. Then I had to drink. Now. My mouth burned like fire. But no one seemed to notice. Strange words I couldn't understand swirled around me. My father was standing tall behind me, talking to a fat man with a shaggy white beard.

My eyes filled with tears. I needed a drink. Bad. I looked down at my full, gathered skirt flaring out about my legs as I stood to reach the table. Quickly, I crammed the edge of the skirt into my mouth. I clenched my teeth on the soothing cotton and rubbed my burning tongue back and forth on the fabric, puffing out my cheeks.

Mama looked at me. "Jewel, don't stuff your skirt in your mouth!" But she knew why. "Chester, the girls really need something to drink," she whispered in English, pulling Papa's head down to hear her above the din of the Ethiopian wedding feast.

A bottle of orange Fanta appeared at my place. A friendly, brown-skinned man popped off the bottle top. It rolled on the dirt floor to the edge of the tent.

The Fanta put out the fire in my mouth so I could eat more spicy stew. A dog nosed under my chair. I threw my chicken bone at him. He wagged his tail and looked up for more. Then it was time to go. Daddy hoisted me on his shoulders. We walked across the hospital compound to our home.

My first memories come from Ethiopia. Our family arrived in 1949, part of a Mennonite mission team of 20-30 North Americans living in five different locations, learning the Amharic language, beginning schools and hospitals.

Mostly I loved romping with Tippy, our dog, climbing the ironwood trees that flanked the road, and playing with my two older sisters. Mama taught us how to read and write while Papa ran a nurse's training school at the mission hospital.

At night, I curled in my crib, pulling the sheet over my head, listening to the hyenas howl and scavenge around town. The worst thing was getting sick with malaria and not knowing if I'd ever get better.

Every Wednesday, we gathered for prayer in the Big House. One night, when we all knelt in a circle to pray -- leaning on our chairs, our knees on the cold cement tile floor, I fell asleep and slid onto the floor. Suddenly, I heard singing. Prayer was over, and everyone was sitting back in their seats. Now, everyone knew I hadn't really been praying. I quickly took my seat. Maybe no one even noticed. Or maybe they knew you could still pray even if you weren't kneeling. They just kept singing, "When the roll is called up yonder, I'll be there." Really, I had been sleeping, not praying, but I think I woke up just in time. Then we ran outside to play No Bears Out Tonight. That was the best part of the prayer meeting.

Dust in a Whirlwind

I was a big girl now. Eight years old and time to go away to boarding school. I sat in the dry grass and watched the tiny whirlwinds dancing around the hospital compound. Dust devils, I called them. They'd catch loose dust, twigs, and trash in swirling funnels. Up, up, and away. Somewhere else far away someone would find my coloring paper.

Tomorrow we'd leave for boarding school. I'd just get picked up and swirled around. Dropped somewhere strange. Why did I have to leave Mama and Papa? But you can't stop the wind. It just comes and carries things away.

Papa said he wished they didn't have to send us away to boarding school. But that was mission policy. Mama could have taught me at home. She wanted to. She was even a trained teacher and had already taught me to read. But if they wanted to be good missionaries, to demonstrate that they loved God more than their family, they had to send us away.

I loved God too, and I know Jesus said some hard things – like that we couldn't love our homes, our mothers, and fathers more than we loved Him. He came first.

At church, I got a new Bible for memorizing verses. I memorized John 3:16, then read the rest of the chapter. It said God's Spirit is like the wind. It blows wherever it wants. We don't know where it comes from or where it goes.

I like the poem Mama read to us. *"Who has seen the wind? Neither you nor I, But when the trees bow down their heads, The wind is passing by. Who has seen the wind? Neither I nor you. But when the leaves hang trembling, The wind is passing through."*

One day at nap time, the wind was so strong it blew our door open. I made up my own little poem: *"Mr. Wind, Mr. Wind, why did you open our door and peek in?"*

I liked the wind. Sometimes it was so strong it blew my braids straight out like flags. But it wasn't strong enough to blow me away like the dust, or was it?

At boarding school, I couldn't be with my family. I wouldn't have a home. But if God wanted me here – if this is where He blew me? Dropped me? What could I do?

But where does wind come from anyway? Mama read us Bible stories before bed. I liked it when it was my turn to sit beside her. I could press her warm, soft leg and see the pictures. A little sailing ship inside big waves. But Jesus told the wind to stop. And it did. Everyone was amazed! No one can control the wind. Houses blow away. Airplanes crash. Ships sink. And all because of the wind.

Mama read about Adam and Eve, too. God made Adam from dust, dirt. But then he blew breath, wind, into his mouth. And he woke up. Became a living man.

I don't want to go to boarding school, but you can't stop the wind! And sometimes the wind is good.

Arrival at Boarding School

Dust swirled behind our VW van. Tiny bits of gravel sprayed up from the wheels. Then Papa slowed down and nosed through a huge flock of sheep and goats that flowed around the van. The angry little goatherd yelled and waved his rod as parts of the flock bolted and headed for a nearby gully. I looked back through the dust as he frantically tried to round up his scattered sheep.

We'd messed up his day. He wasn't happy. But neither was I. Soon we'd be at the boarding school, and I'd have to leave my parents.

Papa parked the van and picked up my suitcase. I clung to Mama's hand and buried my face in her full skirt. The big wooden school door swung open, and a tall lady with thin black hair greeted us. She smiled at Mama, "Welcome to Bingham Academy! So you're the little Mennonite children?"

"I'm Mrs. Wallace, the headmistress here." She smiled, but her face was sharp and scary. When she turned her head, I saw two long pins poked into a tight French twist that snaked up the back of her head.

"The bell's just about ready to ring for supper. That's the dining room...the girls' dormitory is over there...the boys' dormitory is there." She droned on, reciting all the rules to Mama. "This door is only for guests. Wake up at 6:30. Morning prayers at 7. And children mustn't be late, or we might have to dump the cod liver oil in their oatmeal..."

The supper bell rang. Children ran from the dorms, scooting onto backless benches beside long tables.

"Come!" Mrs. Wallace yanked my arm. "You'll sit here with the little girls." My sweaty hand slipped from Mama's grasp. I crowded onto the end of the bench. I could still see Mama and Papa standing just beside the big door. I closed my eyes for prayer. When I opened my eyes, they were gone.

"Pass the bread," an older girl shoved a platter into my hand. "Welcome to hash and trash! You'll soon get used to it."

I wiped my eyes on my dress sleeve. It smelled like dust. Everything was strange. Where was I?

"Now it's time to get changed into PJs before bedtime stories." The older girl, Gloria, coached me. "You'll be my bottom bunker."

That night, I dreamed I was home in my own bed. Mama tucked me in, stopping by my top bunk for a kiss. She smoothed back my hair. Then I jolted awake. Something warm and wet ran down my legs. I'd wet the bed! Terrified, I tented the sheet over my bent knees and drifted back to sleep. In the morning, the sheet was dry. Maybe it was all a dream. I made up the bed.

"Everyone strip off your sheets," Mrs. Wallace said, handing out clean sheets. "Put your top sheets on the bottom and throw your dirty bottom sheets in the laundry pile." Then she saw my sheet with a big yellow splotch. It was mixed in with all the others.

"Who wet the bed?" Her beady black eyes roved the room. No one spoke up. I couldn't. I wouldn't.

"Was it you?" Gloria whispered in my ear. She must have smelled it. "No," I shrugged. "My sheet was dry."

"We don't know," Gloria answered for me. "All our sheets were dry."

"If you ever wet the bed again, don't cover it up," Mrs. Wallace warned. "I'll let it go this time, but never again. Be sure to tell the truth. Don't lie to me!"

Fourteen

Hide and Seek

By Beth Robey Hyde

Hidden World

I was born into a world of contradictions and illusion. My childhood in most ways felt warm, spacious, sunny, and secure. The big house of white-painted brick where my gentle and genteel mother raised my two broters and me; oak and hickory trees in the expansive yard in a peaceful neighborhood where all the neighbor kids played hide-and-seek or kick-the-can on warm summer evenings; extended family close by, some within walking distance; all made for what one might think of as an ideal childhood. Oh, yes. I haven't mentioned the dog; we always had a dog, and the maid. Early on, the maid was a live-in and was almost family; in later years, just a cleaning woman.

In those days before people had phones in hand, folks came and went to people's houses. On Sunday afternoons, ladies made the rounds, visiting friends and leaving calling cards if they called when nobody was home to receive them. Proper visitors came to the front door, and family and servants used the back door.

There were the ice man with his rubber vest and big tongs who brought ice for the refrigerator, the man who asked to paint the house numbers on the curb for a small fee, the knife sharpener who set up his grinder in the driveway and talked all the while he honed the blades that were brought out to him. Mom didn't like the stories he told, and she didn't much like me hanging around him, but I did anyway. When a windowpane broke, a man brought his tools to the house and carefully replaced it with one he had cut to fit. He then put a line of putty around the frame and snugly secured the new one in place. The garbage man emptied the outdoor can into his big one weekly.

There were only edible food scraps and bones in the garbage, carefully wrapped in newspaper. Mr. French then took it to his farm, where it became compost and food for his pigs.

For a while, we had a cleaning woman who was a Choctaw. She told me Indian stories, like the one about why the oak tree keeps its leaves in the winter. *Once there was a poor man who poached a deer from the land of a rich person. He was caught and threatened with death. He begged for mercy and time to say goodbye to his wife and children. The landowner relented and said he would not impose the death sentence until all the leaves were off the trees. The poor man then went to the trees and asked for their help. Only the oak tree responded and agreed to keep its leaves on the tree until the spring, when all the other trees began to sprout new greenery. The poor man was saved, and oak trees still keep their leaves until other trees begin to leaf out in early spring.*

It was not unusual to see someone sitting outside our back door, eating. Mom never turned a hungry person away.

We had a Black yardman who came on a bus all the way from Greenwood once a week to mow, clip, and rake. Mom said it was all right for me to chat with him because he was a minister. His church could not pay him well, so he had to have a business on the side. One day, as I tagged behind him, "helping" by scooping stray leaves onto the growing leaf pile, he commented that he charged my mother less than his other customers because she was a widow. I bless the Rev. Walter Hardin to this day, because he began my education about race, and in doing so, he turned my world upside down. White people who did not live in the South in the days of Jim Crow sometimes do not understand the immensity of this story until I explain that we were the powerful people in the big house on the right side of town, and we were the ones who had the privilege of giving. Walter took power, and as the years went by and I recalled him, my heart broke open.

Sometimes people lived in the "servants' quarters" over the garage. For a short while, there was a grandmother with a grandson about my age. I know nothing about them except that they needed a place to live, and my mother gave it to them. Another time, there was a young woman who was a milliner. She taught me how to make hats and purses. Years later, I remembered her when I made a coat and a purse for my three-year-old daughter. One day, she came into the main house to use the phone, and I belatedly recognized that she was about to deliver a child. When I was a mother myself, my Mom told me the milliner's story: how she was pregnant out of wedlock and her mother had turned her out. Mom said, "When that baby was born, I called the girl's mother and told her it was time for her to come get her child and grandchild and care for them. I had done what was needed, and now it was her turn to step up and act like a mother."

I was born between the great depression and World War II into the Jim Crow South, into an upper-middle-class family. There was great richness for me in the variety of people I encountered, but the conceit of normalcy and respectability formed a curtain that was held together by myriads of true believers and supported by a host of well-bred, well-dressed racist profiteers; much like today, only more polite.

In this mix, I was an observer, in a way sentenced to silence. Conrad Kanagy mentioned that Jesus liked to have the children around him, partly because they were too young to know that their voices were not wanted. I don't think it was entirely because I have ADHD that I have had a life-long inability to speak for myself, but also because society taught me early and well that children, especially girls, should be quiet.

And so I grew, and observed, and yet had the freedom to interact with a far greater variety of people than would likely be possible in today's more structured, more dangerous world. I lived unaware that my privilege was a great jewel taken directly from the hands of less fortunate people, and also that the world I experienced was rapidly disappearing. So while my home life may have been enchanted, some things stemming from it proved real, solid, and lasting.

One was music, the other was church. I was raised on classical and jazz music, sang in choirs and choruses for most of my life, and found joy and consolation through music.

Oh, how fortunate I have been regarding church! Wherever I have lived, the church has been a blessing.

When I recall my childhood at First Christian Church, DOC, a jumble of memories tumbles out like playthings from an overturned toy box. The earliest was of sitting in Sunday School as a 4-year-old when Miss Tricket told us the story of Jesus saying, "Let the little children come to me". I, who had lost my father, looked around the room at the other children and thought, "You had better pay attention. You are going to need Him." Other memories include lemon drops passed to me by my grandmother as I sat in church nestled between her and my mother. I remember my grandfather with other old men wearing criss-cross wrinkles on the backs of their necks above their tight collars as they stood up front and delivered communion prayers, wonderful hymns, my baptism at age 9, when I died and rose again with Jesus, and a sermon about the evils of drunkenness. I recall sitting on the broad front steps of the church, looking down the street to my right, where I saw First Presbyterian and then First Methodist. Across the way was First Baptist, and then to my left up the hill, the queen of churches, Boston Avenue Methodist, reigning over it all. I thought how good it was that these were all Christians!

Everything began to change the summer right after my fifteenth birthday, when my grandfather died. After that came not a jumble but a tangle of memories: my grandmother's descent into deep depression, the death of my dog, the summer I was appointed to accompany Grammy to Chautauqua in the hope it would provide healing for her, my mother's remarriage and our move to Connecticut within days of my 18th birthday and graduation from high school, and then my year at an elite college with a wonderful faculty, in a cold and dark part of the country, my return to Tulsa to live with my brothers and finish college, years back in Connecticut. There, I met and married the man who would be the father of my three children, but the peripatetic life continued as we moved first to the Texas Gulf Coast and then to the Chicago area.

In 1977, I was 40 years old when I began to create my own life story. My mother was critically ill and confined to an intensive care unit. At the same time, my brothers and I took turns flying to Connecticut, they from Tulsa and I from Illinois, to be with her and my stepfather for an interminable three months until her death. Once again, I determined that the clergy, the only outsiders with unlimited access to the ICU, were, in general, doing a terrible job of caring for their parishioners.

So it was that the next autumn, with my husband's spoken agreement, I was in seminary. Thanks, Mom.

Fast-forward to my first pastorate, when we were working on becoming an Open and Affirming congregation. I overheard someone say in a perplexed voice, "Beth likes gay people." The reply came instantly: "Beth likes *people*." Once again, Thanks, Mom.

Seeking Wholeness

Greenwood, the blighted neighborhood where "colored people" lived, lay as far to the north of the city as the prosperous neighborhood where I grew up lay to the south. The oil refinery with its belching smokestacks was across the Arkansas River to the west. Unpleasantness was conveniently screened from our lives, both physically by distance and socially by silence. The help rode buses from Greenwood; the same buses we youngsters took on Saturday afternoons to the neighborhood movie theater to watch John Wayne save hapless and clueless townsfolk from scheming outlaws.

Only some sixteen years before I was born, Greenwood had been known as the Black Wall Street: a community of unprecedented Black prosperity, until that was demolished by White mobs wielding everything from clubs to firebombs because someone thought a Black man had whistled at a White girl.

Was it shame or fear or both that turned that massacre into an unmentionable secret for almost a century? It was never mentioned in any school that I recall, and wasn't discussed at home in front of the children. It wasn't until many years later that we began to hear the words "race riot" spoken aloud, and it wasn't until the year 2000 when a man named Melvin King wrote and published a book titled <u>Tulsa Race Massacre of 1921</u> that its true nature came to public awareness. My older brother had told me in his later years that my beloved grandfather had risked his life by driving repeatedly to Greenwood on the infamous day to bring people to his home for safety. This was the grandfather who had grown up one of 11 siblings on the plantation owned by his parents, and had become a lawyer and one of the founders of a major oil company.

In 2017, a book titled *Killers of the Flower Moon* (subtitled *The Osage Murders and the Birth of the FBI*) was published. Something tugged at my heart as I read it. I recognized the familiar landscape and the names of people and families I had heard my grandfather mention. I wondered how close my family was to that infamous series of events.

Slowly, an old memory resurfaced. I recalled that I had become acquainted with a boy who identified as Osage in high school. My mother had told me that he was a cousin of mine! Aha! Now, perhaps I shall research the name of the family that spoke to me from the pages of a book.

How we hide things from ourselves with those curtains of respectability and normalcy! And how often we fear that speaking the truth will harm us! And how our busyness can make us miss the obvious!

In the year 2016, we were made aware that while we as a nation had become occupied with marginalized minorities, we had unintentionally marginalized others: farmers, miners, male blue-collar workers, rural residents, many of whom still don't have access to the internet. They were angry and hurt and felt not only unseen but also rejected.

We are paying a heavy price for that neglect today. We cannot return to the curtained lives where we naively accepted tree-lined streets, neighbors who spoke to each other, Sundays when everybody in the neighborhood went to church, and hide-and-seek was only a game, as normal.

Six or eight years ago, as cracks were deepening in our society, I was accosted by a casual friend who held to a very traditional view of Christianity. Sadly, he mused, "I don't think I can accept this Emergent Christianity. It pictures God as too lenient. We need not only the carrot but also the stick." I replied, "Have you thought that maybe God is saying that it's time for us to grow up?"

Where we go from here today is a conundrum. But I have learned that whatever we do to others, creatures and even Mother Earth herself, we do to ourselves. I believe this is the essence of the primary instruction in our faith family album: You shall love God and love your neighbor as yourself.

Fifteen

It's Saturday, but
Sunday's Coming

By Charles E. Gardner

It felt like the Saturday between the crucifixion and the resurrection. The negativity of my letter to Tanya seemed overwhelming as I read it to the group last Tuesday night. I had forgotten how bad things had been. Reading aloud brought it back. Having run out of time for discussion, a sense of unease hung over me as we said goodnight to each other. Yet I knew the resurrection was coming, having experienced it in the twenty-two years since the letter was crafted.

I hope that amidst all the pain and sadness described in the letter, the group also perceived the reality that hope is justified even in the worst of circumstances. Over the course of twenty years, from grade school through his mid-twenties, our son Chuck showed progressively worse attitudes and behaviors. They culminated with his assault on his wife, which led to his five years in prison.

A huge irony in all of this is that his time in prison seems to be what led to his healing, and in my mind, his salvation. The very thing that any father would dread is the very thing needed for improvement. He came out of jail with far less anger than when he went in. A dramatic and positive transformation occurred there. While "bumps in the road" have occurred since then, they have been of the nature that we all encounter as we navigate our way in life.

I hope to convey to the group the joy I experience today when I regard our family. One of the happiest days of my life occurred seven years ago, marking the 50th wedding anniversary of Alenda and me. The presence of all of our children and grandchildren, and the love that flowed between us all, was extremely gratifying.

A more recent happy event took place eight months ago, with the birth of our first great-grandchild. A photo on my phone with me, son Chuck, grandson Dalton, and great-grandson Myles brings joy to my heart.

The take home lesson is that God can bring healing to the most badly fractured relationship. It obviously requires forgiveness all around, which Christ tells us we must do to have a right relationship with God. Hope can exist after the crucifixion; the possibility of resurrection is within God's domain.

Eldon Fry grew up in a very rural setting of the Bitterroot Mountains of Idaho, but has spent most of his ministry in university and college contexts. Eldon is ordained and a certified Spiritual Director, providing spiritual direction through Open Hands, a ministry he founded. He has published four books and provides care for his wife, Ginger, who has been diagnosed with Alzheimer's. Eldon is completing a book on the theology of hope, to be published later this year by Santos Books.

Ann King-Grosh has been enriched by her family's experiences, having lived and worked for many years with Mennonite Central Committee and Eastern Mennonite Missions in East Africa. She is now retired and lives with her husband in Lancaster, PA. They are parents of 3 adult children. Ann is involved with welcoming refugees and helping them establish new lives in the Lancaster Community. She is passionate about caring for the earth and volunteers with a local conservancy.

Ted Huffman served for 44 years as a United Church of Christ pastor and teacher, a law enforcement chaplain, and a suicide first responder. Now retired, he is an active grandfather of five, a beekeeper, and a builder of cedar canoes and kayaks. He lives in Northwestern Washington, where the 49th parallel meets the Salish Sea.

Ted is writing a book of prayers and reflections to be published by Santos Books in 2025.

Beth Robey Hyde is a retired pastor in the United Church of Christ. After serving churches in Illinois and Colorado for over 30 years, she is now enjoying a slower pace of life in Northern Illinois as a mother, grandmother, and great-grandmother. Beth is currently writing a manuscript for publication with Santos Books.

Lee Lever is a Vietnam Veteran and retired Mennonite pastor living in Austin, Texas. Chronologically, he has served congregations in Nebraska, Indiana (COB), Washington State, Kansas, and Texas. He is active with the Austin Chapter of Veterans for Peace, volunteers with Interfaith Action of Central Texas, and is a member of a pool team connected with the American Poolplayers Association.

Ruth Martin is a registered nurse. She is most grateful to have lived in the scenic farmland of Lancaster County, PA., all her life. She spends countless hours in her flower garden where the flowers become prayers, and the prayers become flowers. Ruth is currently writing her memoirs for publication with Santos Books.

Edward "Ike" Porter, married to Joy Yutzy Porter and father to Seth, Sean Porter, and Rachel Caluza, served as a pastor in the Mennonite church after receiving an honorable discharge from the U.S. Army. He and his family then served as missionaries with the Mennonite Board of Missions and Voluntary Service, after which he served as a part-time pastor while completing his Master's Degree. He then did a residency in Clinical Pastoral Education. After that, he became a chaplain in a Veterans' hospital, where he became the Chief of Chaplains. He retired from that role to become a pastor in the Church of the Brethren, where he also served as the District Executive of the Michigan District. Ike is working on his memoirs to be published with Santos Books.

Jack Scandrett is a retired Mennonite pastor with 43 years of service. Master's of Divinity in Pastoral Counseling from Anabaptist Mennonite Seminary, Indiana, and a Bachelor's Degree in Biology from Fresno State University, California.

Jewel Showalter resides in an apartment on the campus of Rosedale Bible College in Irwin, Ohio, following a lifetime of international church and mission work alongside her late husband, Richard. She works part-time at the college in development and communications and enjoys spending time with her three married children and their families, including 14 grandchildren. Jewel is finishing her memoirs, which Santos Books will release in the Fall of 2025.

Marc Ian Stewart is a retired United Church of Christ conference minister living in Billings, Montana. He has served with the Montana-N. Wyoming Conference and South Dakota Conference, and as a local church minister in Virginia, Maine, and Michigan. Marc and his spouse, Cheryl Stewart, enjoy kayaking, walking Camino pilgrimages in Spain, Portugal, Italy, and the UK, and spending time with their family.

Cheryl Stewart is currently working as Interim Co-Pastor with her husband, Marc, in Kittery Point, Maine. She enjoys hiking, kayaking, gardening, traveling, playing the piano, and spending time with family and friends.

Charles Gardner grew up in southern New Jersey and worked on his uncle's dairy farm. He attended the College of Agriculture at Cornell from 1967 to 1969, then transferred to the Veterinary College and graduated in 1973. He then joined the Ackermanville Veterinary Hospital, where he primarily practiced dairy cattle medicine. He stayed there until 1989, when he started Dairy Management Consultants, a practice specializing in dairy herd management.

www.ingramcontent.com/pod-product-compliance
Lightning Source LLC
Chambersburg PA
CBHW020416150626
46554CB00014B/1858